THE
BRIDGE
AT DONG HA

**JOHN
GRIDER
MILLER**

**ILLUSTRATIONS BY
KEITH JOHNSTON**

Naval Institute Press   Annapolis, Maryland

9 8 7 6 5 4 3 2 1

Printed in the United States of America

CONTENTS

FOREWORD

*B*ridges have figured prominently in the annals of war. Time and again, the course of history has turned on the destruction or saving of these vulnerable structures so necessary to the transit of armies and supplies. Because of the nature of the work, destruction can frequently be credited to the ingenuity and drive of individual men, whose names abound in both legend and history. What follows is the real story of a Marine Corps hero, John Walter Ripley, who on Easter

Sunday, 1972, almost singlehandedly took on a massive concrete and steel bridge to derail the carefully prepared spearhead attack of the North Vietnamese Army at the Cua Viet River near Dong Ha. For this, he can be compared to the legendary Horatius memorialized by nineteenth-century English historian and poet Thomas Macaulay. In the sixth century B.C. Horatius, virtually unassisted, held back the army of Emperor Tarquin while his Roman soldiers destroyed a bridge over the Tiber River.

Ripley blew up the bridge at Dong Ha by improvisation, swinging hand over hand underneath, dangling from the supporting girders, wrestling boxes of TNT through the channels, bleeding, passing out, ignoring radio chitchat from a distant chain of command about saving the structure for a counterattack. He worked on, despite the sounds and reports of widespread panic as the NVA juggernaut bore down on central South Vietnam, threatening the reorganization of a defense in depth.

John Ripley was an experienced warrior, alone with the courage of his convictions. All the physical and mental and spiritual strength he had built up in a lifetime of service found application on that Easter Day. Horatius would have been lucky to be in his company. The words Thomas Macaulay put into the great Roman's mouth matched the commitment and sensitivity of the John Ripley I know:

> To every man upon this earth
> Death cometh soon or late;

And how can a man die better
Than facing fearful odds
For the ashes of his fathers,
And the temples of his gods?

Ripley's ordeal under the bridge occurred at a time when nearly all Americans had left Vietnam. And like everything else about the war as it dragged on, the results were only halfway gratifying at best. Before another month had elapsed, the North Vietnamese Army had fought its way across upstream bridges to the west, confronted such reinforcements as could be rounded up by the South Vietnamese, and settled for another standoff at the My Chanh River, fifteen miles south of the Cua Viet.

But what a save Ripley made, considering the inevitable had that bridge at Dong Ha been left standing to serve the tank column thundering southward on Easter Sunday! He changed the course of the war. With newly stabilized battle lines, the American bombing resumed in North Vietnam, and it was that effort which ultimately blasted us prisoners of war out of Hanoi. Who knows how things would have come out otherwise? It took the North Vietnamese three years to regroup and prepare for another large-scale invasion.

When Ripley looked at the bridge on Easter morning, he knew exactly how it was constructed because five years earlier he had examined and crossed it time and again. In 1967 he had been fighting near it, along the DMZ, with a regular U.S. Marine Corps unit and thousands of other Americans. In 1972 he was back at the DMZ, this time fighting for his life in a desperate rear-guard action alongside the South Vietnamese. He did so voluntarily. It's easy to give your all when victory appears to be around the corner. The real hero is the man whose sacrifices for his brothers-in-arms come from a sense of sheer duty, even though he knows his efforts are probably doomed to failure.

Surprising to some, perhaps, but it is a fact that men with such a sense of duty are not rare in the U.S. Marine Corps. John came from a Virginia home in which awareness of family heritage and honor was a staple of the nurturing process. That he had ancestors who fought in every American war—including five in the Revolutionary War and some on both sides in the Civil War—was a lesson not lost on him. He served the ashes of his fathers and the temples of his gods. And I write this as one aware of the extra degree of commitment it took for men like him—men who had devoted hard, painful years to the fighting in Vietnam and who could see that America's national resolve was on the wane—to stay the course.

Vice Admiral James B. Stockdale,

U.S. Navy (Retired)

THE BRIDGE AT DONG HA

PROLOGUE

*H*ad it not been for the bridge, the South Vietnamese town of Dong Ha would be remembered today by no one but its own people and the U.S. Marines who fought there in the late 1960s. For years the town, the northernmost one on National Highway 1 in South Vietnam, was little more than a wayside stop serving travelers bound for points north and west. But by the spring of 1972, Dong Ha had become the end of the line. North Vietnamese units were moving freely through the northwestern sector of Quang Tri Province. North of Dong Ha, nothing could be visited without peril. The DMZ—the misnamed demilitarized zone—lay roughly twelve miles in that direction. About the same distance to the west, along National Highway 9, a former U.S. Marine Corps base called Camp Carroll guarded South Vietnam's northwest flank. Camp Carroll was garrisoned by the Fifty-Sixth Regiment of the ARVN, the Army of the Republic of Vietnam.

Dong Ha squatted along the south bank of the Cua Viet River, which flowed eastward from the narrow headwaters of the Cam Lo River. Swollen by the winter monsoon, the Cua Viet measured five hundred feet wide when it surged past Dong Ha toward the South China Sea ten miles away. Small boats in the river had to contend with a swift current and fast-moving debris.

In 1967, SeaBees from a U.S. Navy construction battalion built a two-lane highway bridge across the Cua Viet to meet the growing demands of military traffic up and down Highway 1, the country's only north-south artery. An old French-built bridge just upstream had become inadequate for military purposes, as had a heavily damaged railroad bridge farther upstream, whose spans lay rusting in the river.

While the SeaBees were building their bridge, the U.S. Marines operated from a combat base adjacent to Dong Ha. It became the logistic hub of the area, providing support for fifty thousand men fighting along the DMZ. With a short airstrip, dirt at first, later covered with runway matting, it handled light aircraft and propeller-driven cargo planes as well as damaged jets returning from strikes in North Vietnam. The base was their first haven in friendly territory. Soon after it was established, the North Vietnamese Army—the NVA—brought Dong Ha within range of its heavy artillery. In time, after severe shelling, the Americans decided to move south out of artillery range, and so they abandoned the base to the elements.

By the spring of 1972 nearly all the Americans in Vietnam, at one time more than half a million, had left the country. U.S. Navy warships still patrolled the coastline, and some U.S. aircraft flew overhead. But the only Americans that remained in ground combat were the Marine Air and Naval Gunfire Liaison Company's (ANGLICO's) forward observers, who coordinated fire support for the Vietnamese, and a dwindling number of advisors to South Vietnamese combat units.

Since other American ground units were unlikely to be reintroduced, the North Vietnamese were now free to step up military activity and deal with the Southerners in their own way. Their timetable had been disrupted by American and South Vietnamese military thrusts into Cambodia and Laos in 1970 and 1971, operations that helped cover the general withdrawal of U.S. units from the war theater as the conflict became "Vietnamized." Despite delays, however, the NVA buildup was complete by

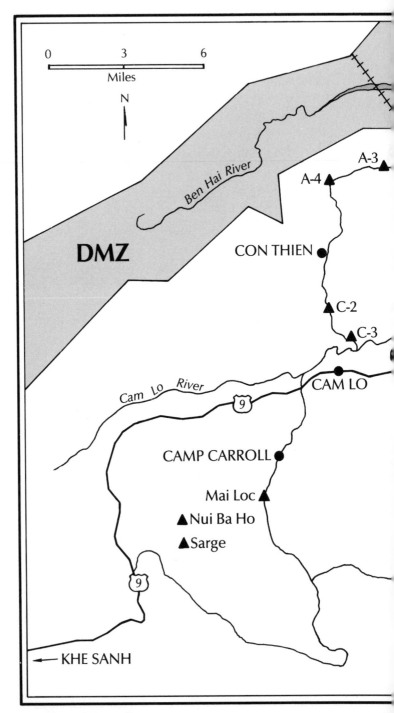

Dong Ha and vicinity

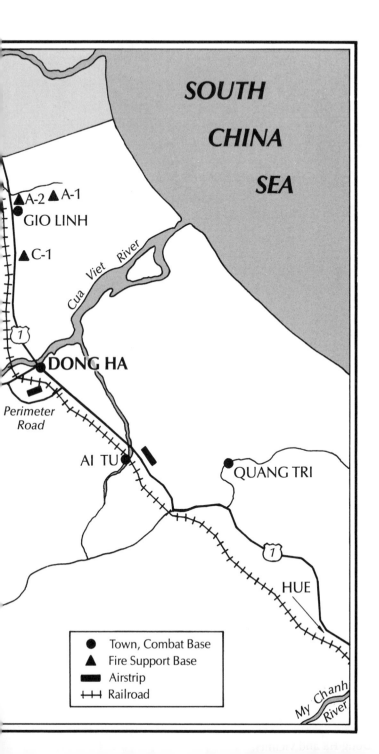

the spring of 1972. One large-scale attack, part of a multi-pronged assault on South Vietnam, would come across the DMZ. Two infantry divisions, nearly thirty thousand soldiers counting armor and artillery support, were poised to attack south along Highway 1. They hoped to develop momentum for a push all the way to the gates of Vietnam's ancient imperial capital, Hue City, thirty miles beyond Dong Ha.

The NVA's 308th Division was placed in the vanguard of the attack. Victorious in the decisive campaign of the Vietminh (Indochina) War in 1954, the 308th had received the ultimate battle honor, that of accepting the surrender of the French garrison at Dien Bien Phu. After that the division served as a gold-plated palace guard in Hanoi, sitting out the ensuing years of struggle.

Now, after nearly eighteen years, this elite force was ready to enter combat again. In their thrust down the coastal plain, the Northerners first needed to overrun the handful of South Vietnamese artillery fire bases just south of the DMZ. Then they would have to seize the highway bridge at Dong Ha and keep men and material moving south over the first major water obstacle, the Cua Viet River.

The Third ARVN Division was charged with defending the region. It consisted of newly formed ARVN regiments and two brigades of the South Vietnamese Marine Corps, the VNMC. Thinly spread, the defenders operated from isolated artillery bases, strongpoints, and outposts, not from a continuous line of defensive positions that could support each other by fire. The Army units in the Third Division were filled with untested troop leaders, uncertain staff officers, and men whose fighting spirit was flagging. Some of the division's soldiers had deserted from other ARVN units. Apprehended and punished, they were then reassigned near the DMZ because there were fewer places to desert to that far north.

In sharp contrast, the division's VNMC brigades were battle-hardened. Throughout the long war they had consistently taken the fight to the enemy, most recently in Cambodia and Laos. They were veterans of many tough campaigns, descendants of the French river assault groups that operated during the Vietminh War. They had seen few days of peacetime service in their eighteen-year history. Besides fighting against the Viet Cong and the NVA, they had been tasked at various times to confront such home-grown threats as the armies of the militant Cao Dai and Hoa Hao sects and the Binh Xuyen river and coastal pirates.

In structure the VNMC was patterned only loosely after the U.S. Marines, but in training and tactics it followed its model closely. The obstacle course at the Di An recruit training center, for example, was a close copy of the one at Parris Island in South Carolina, scaled down to accommodate the smaller Vietnamese. VNMC drill instructors supervised training and administered discipline with a full-scale measure of Marine Corps intensity and occasional ferocity. Some of these noncommissioned officers had been to Parris Island themselves for schooling. In addition, many key officers received at least one year's advanced training with their U.S. counterparts at Quantico. Most of these officers spoke English well and had a good grasp of Marine Corps tactics, weapons, and battle doctrine.

Along with the Airborne and Ranger divisions, the Marines constituted South Vietnam's elite national reserve. Though as a rule a reserve force is held back initially and later enters combat only to exploit battlefield successes or to save desperate defensive situations, two-thirds of the "reserve" VNMC were fully engaged. They had been operating in Quang Tri Province since the beginning of the Laotian cross-border operation, Lam Son 719, more than a year earlier.

After preliminary artillery attacks and infantry probes, the NVA launched its 1972 Easter Offensive on 30 March. The commanding general of the Third ARVN Division ordered the Third VNMC Battalion to leave fire-support base Barbara, south of Quang Tri City, and travel by night truck convoy to Dong Ha. Upon arrival, it would receive further orders.

The Third Battalion was still ostensibly uncommitted and therefore remained the reserve force of the Third ARVN Division. In reality, however, the 700-man battalion was the only infantry unit in position to plug that critical artery, the highway bridge over the Cua Viet. If South Vietnamese forces were to have any chance of organizing a defense-in-depth for Quang Tri Province, the Third Battalion would have to stop the NVA at Dong Ha.

The battalion completed its nighttime motor march during the early-morning hours of Good Friday. New orders had not yet arrived, but the battalion's implicit mission was becoming clearer with each passing hour. The invasion force continued its steady advance, surrounding and overrunning outposts and fire-support bases on the way to Dong Ha.

The prospective defenders of Dong Ha were first-rate, one of the finest units in the VNMC. The Marines of the Third Battalion wore shoulder patches that identified them as the Soi Bien, Wolves of the Sea. They had recently rested and been restored to full strength after a month-long stand-down period at Di An, their base camp near Saigon.

During the six months of operations along the DMZ that immediately preceded the stand-down, the Third Battalion had been hard hit, with nearly forty percent of its Marines killed or wounded in combat. The ranks had been further thinned by illness attributed to the cold rains of the winter monsoon. Recruited from Saigon and points south, where there is no winter, many Marines adapted poorly to the cold and perpetual dampness of winter in Vietnam's middle region. Their uniforms and boots, seldom if ever completely dry, rotted and fell apart. They also adapted poorly to the change in diet. Marines had to procure food locally, and the difficulty of that task increased dramatically as their distance from the Mekong Delta rice bowl increased. Meat and fish were particularly hard to obtain. In time, protein deficiencies developed and Marines began to suffer chills and fever, symptoms initially and incorrectly diagnosed as malaria. In any event, the victims were just as hard hit as malaria victims and had to be evacuated. Their quick recovery in hospitals baffled doctors until they discovered the link to diet and prescribed protein supplements.

So after six months of field duty even the hardiest Marines required stand-down periods, which gave them respite from a war that completely dominated their young lives. On leave, the men had a chance to enjoy precious visits with families and friends, interludes that restored their spirits, though they knew that inevitably they would have to return to the hardships and anxieties of combat. Most did go back, but not all.

Thus primed for new challenges after its stand-down, the Third Battalion had been at fire base Barbara less than a week before it received the order to move north. Commanding the unit was Major Le Ba Binh, who had begun his military career in the Third Battalion. Binh's personal combat record was remarkable by anyone's standards. He believed in leading his men from the front. Decorated many times over and wounded on a dozen occasions, he was held in awe by his men.

No one respected Binh more than his U.S. Marine Corps advisor, his *co-van*, Captain John Walter Ripley of Radford, Virginia. Ripley had made a lifelong habit of tackling tough assignments. With marginal academic qualifications, he entered the U.S. Naval Academy after Parris Island and enlisted service, taking on the school's heavy load of science, mathematics, and engineering in a four-year struggle for an officer's commission. Surviving those years taught him that no system could beat him if he did not let it. And there were some bright moments. Early Marine Corps training gave him an edge in physical fitness. He led his class in first-year tests of applied strength and agility, and developed skills in gymnastics, boxing, wrestling, and swimming. The gymnasium offered respite from the demands of study, recitation, inspection, and testing.

Ripley logged a lot of infantry time during his ten years as a Marine officer. In 1967 he led a rifle company of the Third U.S. Marine Division through almost a year of intense combat along the DMZ. Wounded in action and evacuated at one point, he managed to return to his company in time to regain command for the rest of his tour in Vietnam. Later, during an exchange tour of duty with Great Britain's Royal Marines, he commanded a rifle company in the battalion-sized Forty-Five Commando. After special training at the U.S. Army's Airborne and Ranger schools, and with the frogmen of the U.S. Navy's underwater demolition teams, Ripley also served with a Marine Corps force reconnaissance company. This elite unit specialized in clandestine inserts into hostile areas, either by parachute or from the sea, using submarines and small boats. The recon Marines, trained in such exotic tasks as demolitions and mountain climbing, kept themselves in splendid physical condition by swimming, running, and hiking over long distances.

The thirty-two-year-old Ripley stood five feet

eleven and weighed 175 pounds. Like most of the other advisors, he quickly shed ten pounds after starting the Vietnamese rice-and-roots diet. He still looked and felt gargantuan whenever he stood alongside the slightly built Binh, but the physical difference was about the only one they had. The two enjoyed a close, hand-in-glove relationship, part of a tradition that dated back to the first U.S. advisor—who helped form the VNMC in 1954—and produced the term *co-van*, meaning "trusted friend." Their friendship and mutual respect was a result of Ripley's decrypting the Vietnamese way of doing things, which remained a mystery to many Americans even after months or years of close association with their Asian hosts. Not all Vietnamese Marine commanders sought or took advice from less-experienced American counterparts, who were usually less senior in rank as well. Some senior officers developed strong anti-American feelings that steadily hardened as total U.S. disengagement from South Vietnam became more and more certain. Their *co-vans* were in a perpetual no-win situation.

More often the Vietnamese commanders were friendly, but each new advisor still had to prove himself, usually under fire, to gain trust and respect. In Ripley's case acceptance came early. Binh knew that the American's earlier combat experiences at Khe Sanh and Con Thien matched or surpassed his own. At this stage of the war, moreover, most Vietnamese appreciated the fact that Ripley and other American Marines were volunteers. They had sought advisory assignments instead of service with U.S. Marine infantry battalions that had been withdrawn months earlier. The *co-van*s didn't have to be in Vietnam, but they were, anyway—each man for his own reasons.

By Easter morning the North Vietnamese offensive was nearing its initial objectives in Quang Tri. As dawn approached, two NVA infantry divisions spearheaded by a large tank column were closing in on Dong Ha. North Vietnamese artillery fire, sporadic at first, now rained on the town and the adjacent combat base with steadily increasing intensity, driving the defenders under cover. The invaders appeared determined to reduce Dong Ha to a graveyard, leaving no one alive to resist when the time came to send tanks across the river. Their penchant for caution was strong even when the balance of forces weighed heavily in their favor, and their combat experience with tanks was limited.

In a matter of hours, Dong Ha would become the focal point of the world's attention. Like Bastogne, or Gettysburg, or the Alamo, the site itself encompassed little of importance. But the events beginning to unfold there would come to matter a great deal to a great many people.

ONE

*T*he artillery round made a truncated scream just before it landed with the crumping sound and concussion of colliding freight cars. Loose dirt sifted from the rafters of the cinder-block building and settled over him in a fine layer. He was curled up in a poncho liner hoping for sleep in this last hour of darkness. His stomach muscles tightened, trying to keep fear inside until the danger passed. It would only be seconds before the next round hit.

That gunner has me in his pocket, Ripley thought. And he's not going to quit until he kills me.

He could always go to sleep to the sound of his own guns, American or South Vietnamese. The crash of 105-millimeter howitzers or the sharper, louder crack of 155s would be followed by the comforting whoosh-and-rumble of rounds on their way to punish and disorient a distant foe. But incoming was a lot different. Almost without warning—just that short scream before impact—the enemy was on top of you.

Rounds were coming in four or five each minute and the screams they made were getting louder and shorter. What would happen when one landed without a scream? Bull's-eye. Would he even feel it happen? If God had any mercy, no. He'd just wake up dead. Or maybe crushed in the rubble, fighting for a few last gasps of air. What a miserable prospect, he thought.

The heavier, longer-range guns of the North Vietnamese Army had driven the Southerners under cover. Their return fire was weak between incoming rounds and their shorter-range guns could barely reach the forwardmost NVA positions.

The shelling had kept up for two days and nights, ever since he and the South Vietnamese Marines moved into this abandoned combat base. It had been dark when Binh picked the building for his command post but Ripley had recognized it. Five years earlier, when fifty thousand U.S. Marines had occupied the base, this was the Third Marine Division morgue. Now with only a battalion in the area it was the one building left intact. The scavengers wouldn't touch this home of tortured spirits, victims of violent death. He wasn't going to tell Binh what it used to be. Binh was new to the area and Ripley didn't want to spook him.

The place still stank of death, that cloying, almost-sweet smell that hit a man like a whiff of ammonia. He could still see the transfer cases stacked neatly on the loading dock. When he and Binh had first entered the building, he instinctively sidestepped the spot where they once sat.

As a morgue, the room had been starkly lit. Unshaded bulbs dangled overhead and grew dim whenever the generator outside faltered. The graves registration people, moon shadows under their eyes, worked with silent efficiency as they prepared the bodies of young Marines for their final journey home.

He remembered the mangled men, the faces contorted in death, the bodies that no longer had faces. Some still had tubes running out of them, evidence of futile lifesaving attempts. Bloody, mud-caked weapons and equipment were pushed aside from time to time to make room for more bodies, and more bodies, and still more bodies. Litters were soaked with blood, and a stinking mixture of medicine and body fluids had spread over the floor and made it slippery. Ragged jungle uniforms lay in piles, cut away from their owners, young men returned to the nakedness of birth and denied their dignity in death. And then there were the greenish body bags, the color of death. Airtight, filling with the gases of decomposition, growing and growing with the shiny puffiness of engorged leeches.

It all came back so clearly, as if there were no years separating this moment from the last time he'd been here. He had to block it out. He pulled his poncho liner over his face, then wished he hadn't. He smelled like a goat.

The room was getting lighter. He could make out clusters of men sleeping or trying to. He rolled on his side and drew his knees up in one final attempt to stave off the incoming's screams and bring on sleep. He closed his eyes but it was useless.

When he opened them again it was lighter still and Three-Finger Jack was staring at him. Binh's senior bodyguard was bigger than most Vietnamese, with a big head and big hands and a powerful build. His facial features were roughhewn and his cheekbones sat high in his squarish face, as uncharacteristically Vietnamese as his thick black mustache. But it was his eyes that made the strongest impression. Hooded, unblinking, expressionless as a shark's, they sat watchful over a fathomless and perpetual half-smile, softening only in the presence of trusted friends. Jack had a hardness that had been bred through generations of warriors. He could have ridden with Genghis Khan or the revered savior of Vietnam, Tran Hung Dao.

Ripley admired the man without understanding him. That transfixing gaze was fearless; he wondered if it could read any of his own fears.

He rolled over and thought of his family, the bright, still place inside that brought peace even when the outside world seemed to be closing in to crush him. He patted his breast pocket and the small plastic-wrapped package that held snapshots of them. At home in the Blue Ridge mountains they were as far from this hell as they could possibly be, on the other side of the world. It was easy to figure the time back there—just turn this morning into the previous evening. They'd be at dinner, talking about the Easter bunny. He thought of the kids getting out of bed Easter morning and running to their baskets. Then a thought rolled in that he had been trying to avoid: In a few more hours he could be dead, face down in the mud, and the kids would never know it, eating their chocolate eggs and dumping their baskets to be sure they'd found all the candy. They existed back there in a perfect world he would never return to, cut off from them forever. No one would be able to tell them what had happened, much less explain what it meant. And who could explain to his parents why they'd lost their second son in a year?

It had been ten months since he'd seen his family. He'd been on leave, back from Malaya and the wrap-up of his tour with the Royal Marines. Most of the U.S. servicemen were out of Vietnam by then, but he had orders to go back as an advisor, a *co-van*. He returned on a chartered airliner like a tourist. Despite barbed wire and sandbags on the streets, Saigon had lost its look of wartime urgency. His walk from the Splendid Hotel to the white-washed Vietnamese Marine headquarters compound took him along shaded residential streets, away from the fumes of pop-popping motorbikes on Tu Do Street downtown. During his in-briefings at the compound, shouts from the courtyard outside told him that his American and Vietnamese counterparts were putting the war on hold long enough for their daily volleyball game.

Less than a week later, uncomfortable in a satiny new tiger suit with a spiky camouflage pattern, he began his trek to the DMZ to join the Third Marine Battalion. The airstrips at Da Nang, Phu Bai, and Quang Tri were operating at a fraction of their earlier capacity. The short strip at Dong Ha had been closed for many months. From Quang Tri, he had to go by helicopter.

During the low-altitude flight he saw familiar terrain: trails leading to remote hilltops that had been scraped clean for artillery positions, others that ran along barren ridgelines and suddenly disappeared into forested valleys. The U.S. Marines had renamed the areas of heaviest fighting. No-Drink Creek was a stream with bodies piled so high they dammed it up, creating a small pond. Skull Orchard didn't take much imagination to figure out. And Fried Rice had nothing to do with rice; the name of that trail junction was inspired by maggots.

Five years earlier Ripley's company had spent eleven months around here, along the DMZ. Nearly everyone became a casualty; the company lost two full sets of officers. He himself was wounded in a night-long melee that took out half the company, but also put an NVA regimental command group and its security forces out of action.

Back then the DMZ had been unbearable. Marines who headed south at the end of year-long tours were reddened—branded—by the clay that ground itself into their uniforms, boots, equipment, hair, skin, and eyes. But at least there were fifty thousand of those Marines fighting along the DMZ and they were winning. Now with only seven hundred, how could they hold the line? He couldn't talk to an American face to face. The *co-vans* were scattered, no more than two per battalion and sometimes one. He wondered about the two assigned to the Fourth Battalion, which had been surrounded and driven off fire-support bases Sarge and Nui Ba Ho directly to the west. The advisors were probably with the battalion's Alpha and Bravo command groups trying to evade the encircling North Vietnamese as they moved across rugged terrain. But no one had heard. When would it be the Third Battalion's turn to face encirclement?

A cold more penetrating than the morning's damp chill started moving up his legs and he felt as though he were being lowered into a well. The docs said a man died from the feet up. Had it started? Was he setting himself up for his own death? He was convinced that some people did. Call it premonition, self-fulfilling prophecy. After a while on the line you could almost tell who was going to get it. Everyone knew that.

He pulled the poncho tighter around him and tried to empty out his head. Get some sleep, he thought. But it was almost daylight and his mind was still racing. They were going to need help today. Where would it come from? Most of the Americans were gone. Was Dong Ha now as unreal to the United States as the family in his snapshots had become to him? Didn't anybody know what was going on up here? Did they care?

No one could answer him. He was in a dark morgue surrounded by Marines who spoke no English. The only other noise besides incoming artillery was the steady rushing of his tactical radio, unbroken for hours by voice transmissions.

There were a dozen men in the room—Binh, his operations officer, the radio operators, the bodyguards, and the cowboys who set up and broke camp. They started and turned with each new explosion, but still they were sleeping. They didn't seem to worry much about death. Maybe they were used to the idea. Binh had been wounded a dozen times. He wasn't sweating out a one-year tour and going home; he was in it until the end. For him and for all the Vietnamese Marines the only honorable way out was feet first.

No more of this thinking. He threw aside his poncho and stood up. Three-Finger Jack was stroking the stubble on his face with the stump of a missing forefinger, watching him with that odd half-smile like someone with superior knowledge, privately amused. He must like *some*thing about me, Ripley thought, nodding and starting toward the doorway.

He'd first seen him months earlier at Khe Sanh, near the Laotian border. Jack had been the newest of Binh's three bodyguards. The senior one was feeling threatened. Ripley smelled bad blood; a showdown was inevitable.

The two bodyguards faced each other, tense and alert. Jack's senior began a stream of abuse. "You are undeserving. No courage. You have nothing in your pants."

Jack moved closer, eyes expressionless, the cobra stalking the flustered bird. The senior bodyguard continued, his voice climbing a full octave. "Nobody trusts you. When you came here, nobody smiled. *Thieu-ta* Binh does not trust you. Your loyalty is not pure."

Jack approached the bodyguard until they stood face to face. Deliberately, he reached for his fighting knife and slid it from its scabbard. The other man fell silent, transfixed. Jack showed him the six-inch blade, a magician displaying his handkerchief before the trick. Without changing expression or looking away he wrapped the forefinger of his left hand around the blade and squeezed. Blood welled from the cut and ran down the blade to the hilt.

Jack was in command. He paused. His smile grew confident, triumphant, arrogant; his lips curled back to reveal a slight gap between his two front teeth. Then in one quick motion he ripped the blade back and up. Severed cleanly, the finger went flying, blood arcing behind it.

Ripley had approached Jack woodenly, in someone else's body, pulling his green mesh sweat rag from around his neck. Jack sheathed his fighting knife and took the rag, pressing it against the bloody stump and keeping his eyes fixed on his antagonist. Then he held the mutilated hand in the other man's face and spoke.

"Today, I cut off my finger for *Thieu-ta* Binh. Someday, I die for him."

Two days later they found the corpse of the senior bodyguard. His throat had been slit and his own knife had been plunged into his chest up to the hilt.

Jack became senior bodyguard.

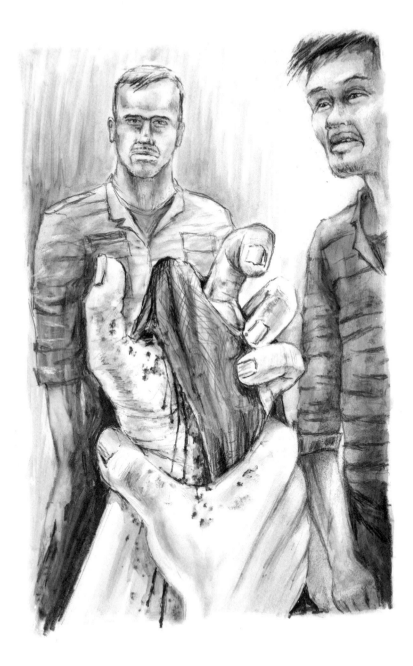

TWO

*I*t was Easter morning and a chill overcast carried the threat of more rain. He was watching the pale sunrise, glad to be out of the morgue. He could get his bearings here.

The landscape looked like a junkyard on the moon. In a nearby field a Phantom fighter-bomber that had overshot the runway years before lay in decay. Vehicle parts and barbed wire rusted, half-buried, in the mud. Sandbags that had not been burst open by artillery fire were rotting, their contents bleeding down the bunkers' sides. The treeless ground, a dusty hardpan during the dry months, was soaked from the winter monsoon and any vehicle that skidded off the rain-slick road risked getting mired up to its axles in red clay. The stuff could suck the boots off a soldier trying to cross it on foot. Craters pockmarked the terrain. Nearly all the buildings had been cannibalized—stripped of corrugated tin roofing, plywood, electrical wiring. Only the old morgue was left untouched.

The shelling continued but the sound of exploding rounds was fading. They were shifting fire away from the base and toward town. Why? Surely they knew the base hadn't been abandoned.

He ran his hand across the stubble on his face and listened to his slack belly growl. Normally, when he and his radioman Nha weren't away from the command group, he ate with Binh. It had been a long time since their last meal. They would usually have a small bowl of rice late in the morning and another early in the evening, an hour or so before dark. Sometimes they sprinkled small pieces of pork or fish on top of the rice and ate fruit for dessert. One of Binh's cowboys would call Ripley to the meal. "*An com, Dai-uy.*" Eat rice, Captain. It was always the same chow call, whether the meal was going to be rice or, if they were having a party, something else. They never ate rice with their party food.

The Vietnamese didn't take breakfast in the field, but the cowboys would give a *co-van* a break when they could. They might fix him a wakeup bowl of

Chinese noodles, draining off enough hot water for a cup of chicory-flavored Vietnamese coffee.

He thought about all the rice and roots he'd put away over the years and wished that he could strap on a nice, thick steak for a change, though the last time he'd tried one back in Saigon his system hadn't been able to take it. He'd been sick as a dog. Still, he longed for a steak, and for coffee and thick sweet cream and one of the French rolls his cowboy sometimes scared up for him when they were near a town. But there wouldn't be time to scrounge for food today; and even if there were, they had no dry wood, no clean water, nothing.

Nha was staring at him. Baby-face Nha, with his sad eyes and open, trusting smile. Never far away, never without his Prick 77, the AN/PRC-77 radio he carried on his back as though it were part of his anatomy. Nha and his radio were inseparable, just like Nha and Ripley. For months they had shared the same fighting hole, the same poncho, the same rice bowl. Neither knew the other's language well, but facial expressions and body language made words unnecessary. Nha could read his mind. He was his *anh nho*. His little brother. His gutsy little brother.

It was odd that a man with almost no English served as his sole link with the outside world. His only way to stay in contact with the people who could save them—with artillery, naval gunfire, air strikes. The only ones who could send reinforcements.

Nha approached with his long-range whip antenna waving like a fly rod. Fifteen feet long, it served as a beacon for enemy marksmen; he couldn't have drawn more attention with a brass band. But most of the time his job required the long antenna. That was why radiomen got hit early, like machine-gunners, and that was why the undistinguished-looking Nha had everybody's respect.

Nha handed the radio handset to Ripley, who remembered that he owed Brigade an overnight report. Brigade 258 had set up its command post at Ai Tu, six miles to the south.

He fingered the handset. "Leatherneck, this is Delta. Over."

"Where you been, Delta, sleeping in?" Sometimes the chatter got loose on the *co-van* radio net.

"Too noisy. We took three or four rounds a minute all night long. I'll get you a casualty count when the rifle companies report in."

"Roger. Anything else?"

"I'm going to do a crater analysis on some new shell holes, find out where the bastards are shooting from."

"Roger. Nothing else?"

"Negative at this time. Out."

"Roger, out."

What did he mean, nothing else, Ripley wondered, annoyed. He wouldn't mind some information flowing downhill for a change. What was the reason for all this heavy incoming? And what was happening to the Fourth Battalion?

He gave the handset back to Nha and began to

look for fresh shell holes. They weren't hard to spot after a rain. The newest ones held the least water, and for several minutes after an explosion they would give off wisps of smoke from burning powder and cordite and whatever they'd hit. He pulled his compass from its pouch and lay down beside one of the elliptical shell holes. The acrid smell made his nostrils burn as he sighted down the crater's long axis and took his compass reading of the direction of fire. Then he moved to another new hole, then another, and plotted the readings on his tactical map. The lines intersected north of Con Thien, thirteen miles to the northwest.

Con Thien? The North Vietnamese usually fired artillery from Dong Ha Mountain or Helicopter Valley, west of Con Thien, from deep cover in the wooded areas. But now they'd moved their heavy artillery onto the coastal plain, where it was vulnerable to return fire and air strikes if the weather lifted. They couldn't be worried about counterbattery fire any more. And they were burning up ammunition as if there were no tomorrow, so their ammo must have been staged forward, too. They would keep leapfrogging artillery farther and farther east and south to cover the tanks rolling down Highway 1 and they'd be on top of the Third Battalion in no time.

He had to call this in. Brigade should know.

But Brigade radioed first. Nha came running with the handset extended. He looked worried. He could sense urgency on the radio net without understanding all the words. "Stand by for something big," the message came crackling through. "Soon. Out."

He couldn't be annoyed at Brigade's brushoff this time. The *co-van*s back there were probably covering half a dozen nets at once. Something was happening, finally. Then Brigade came back on. "Orders are coming down the ARVN chain. Fall back on Dong Ha and defend the bridge site. I'll give you more when I can. Out."

Three-Finger Jack appeared, looking for him. Binh had already received the order to fall back and wanted the *co-van* in his command post. Ripley, Nha, and Jack ran back to the morgue.

Binh was young, in his early thirties, with a slight build and smooth skin that gave him an almost boy-ish look from the neck up. The rest of him testified to a career of stoic endurance. Ripley had seen it nearly a year earlier, at Khe Sanh, when the battalion command group stopped to bathe in a mountain stream. The Vietnamese hated to disrobe in front of Americans, but after several days of combat they had no choice but to wash in Ripley's presence. With stiff, formal movements, Binh removed his tiger suit. And Ripley, trying not to stare, saw in one sweeping glance the shiny white blotches and purple rope-like welts running over Binh's back, chest, and limbs. Quick fixes under the field surgeon's knife.

He'd been wounded twelve times and decorated with seven Crosses of Gallantry and awarded the National Order, Knight's Class. A Vietnamese samurai, aristocratic warrior class, contender for commandant if he survived this war. His Marines rallied to his leadership; when wounds took him out of action and command fell to a subordinate, they tended to run ragged and leaderless.

Binh had wasted no time. When Ripley reached the morgue he said, "I have alerted two rifle companies and the Alpha command group, and they are ready to move at once. The other two companies and the Bravo command group are still out of radio contact." They were operating with an ARVN tank battalion, somewhere along the five-mile stretch of Highway 9 between Dong Ha and Cam Lo. "*Dai-uy* Ripley, *s'il vous plaît*, I want you to walk to Highway 9 with me and link up with the rest of the battalion."

"I'm ready," Ripley said. "*Chung toi di ra di.*" Let's get going.

The Alpha command group had already left the morgue and formed into a column. Ripley and Binh moved to the front and started for Dong Ha and Highway 9. Within minutes, Nha approached with the handset. Brigade again.

"A bombshell. No time for questions. Confirmed by Mark I eyeball sightings. Expect enemy tanks. Out."

"Tanks," Ripley said, turning to Binh. "Godalmighty damn. How many do you think? A platoon? A battalion?"

Binh tried to conceal his surprise. He usually heard first, over his own radio net. "Any more than five, we cannot handle. We have only ten light anti-tank weapons. Ten rounds. My Marines have never shot at tanks. They do not know how to attack them."

Ripley nodded. "I think they have a lot more than five tanks. We've got a problem."

Binh summoned his radioman and gave orders for the two available rifle companies to deploy along the south bank of the Cua Viet River and start digging in. One company would cover the main bridge used by north-south traffic along Highway 1. It had been built by the SeaBees five years earlier to carry the heaviest American weapons and equipment, including tanks and self-propelled artillery pieces. The other company would cover the older, smaller French-built bridge just upstream, which handled nothing heavier than light wheeled vehicles.

He ordered each rifle company to put a hundred Marines in firing positions along the riverbank, covering a frontage of four hundred yards. They were to dig their holes deep and there would be no fallback positions. They had to hold the riverbank.

If anyone can hold, it's the Third Battalion, thought Ripley. The Soi Bien, Wolves of the Sea. A year earlier in Laos they had fought their way up Co Roc Ridge, twice the height of Gibraltar. Under heavy pressure they pulled off Co Roc at night, bringing the dead and wounded down sheer cliffs in the tradition of their U.S. Marine counterparts. Outnumbered greatly by the encircling North Vietnamese, they had battled their way back to Khe Sanh, again taking the dead and wounded.

The command group reached Highway 9 only to find it clogged with refugees fleeing the guns and the threat of invasion. It was hard working against the heavy flow of people. Their heads were weighed down by the fear of death and they stared silently at the ground, keeping stubbornly on track, blocking out anything that didn't appear in that little spot before them. They suffered no longer as individuals but as one massive herd with a single goal: to get as far away as possible as quickly as possible. To do this, they were leaving the only place Vietnamese souls could find rest, alongside ancestors. With heads bowed, they were walking into purgatory.

"How many do you think there are?" Ripley asked Binh.

Binh was looking westward past the refugees, as if it pained him to see them. But his voice was flat and emotionless. "Thirty, forty thousand, maybe. The whole valley is moving."

Despite the numbers and the fear and the confusion families managed to stay together—fathers pulling loaded carts if they were rich enough to have them, less fortunate ones pushing bicycles with their life's belongings lashed on; mothers balancing heavy baskets on springy dum-dum sticks; young girls with infants on their backs, followed by elders trying to keep up and carrying something if they could; and bringing up the rear, boys too young for military service leading livestock or helping those who stumbled.

Ripley had never seen refugees in such numbers before. We're the only ones in uniform they see, he thought. The only ones carrying weapons. Two big dogs fighting in their yard are making them move, and we're the only dog they can see.

They were nearly out of Dong Ha. In a small house beside the highway a family was holding a funeral. The front wall of the house was torn away and the interior opened like a stage set onto the crowd, making a show of the family's ritual of grief. The dead man lay on a table in the center of the main room. A dirty sheet covered all but the soles of his feet, which faced the highway. The family gathered around the table crying and chanting, weaving from side to side in grief. There had not been time to prepare; the burning joss sticks, the framed portrait of the deceased, the white shirts and *ao dai*s that usually went with Vietnamese funerals—all were missing.

Ripley was troubled. The children were no older than his own and they'd been left behind by their father to survive this. How could they? How many American kids could? Would his own kids have to survive without him? And it came to him moving against the refugees that he was one with them, absorbing their despair as he pushed his way through it—a man suddenly with no past, no identity, just a trapped soul trying to escape into the future and getting nowhere.

Then in the stream of civilians men of military age began to appear. Dark splotches on their faded ARVN uniforms showed that name tags, unit patches, and insignia of rank had recently been

removed. They carried no military equipment—no weapons or ammunition, no helmets, no hats, not even canteens.

"Look at them," Ripley said bitterly. "Deserters."

The men walked by silently, eyes fixed straight ahead. They looked naked and vulnerable as though they, like their uniforms, had been stripped of all the trappings of pride and position until there was nothing left but this blind and overpowering instinct to move south.

B*inh wasn't even looking at them—he was still staring west over the heads of the crowd—but his neck muscles were taut and his jaw worked as he gritted his teeth. He held his hands free of his sides, like a gunfighter out of the Old West.

If they were Marines he'd tear them apart, Ripley thought. He remembered what had happened at fire base Alpha 2, up north at Gio Linh. A young Marine on leave had decided not to return to the Third

Battalion. The White Mice—the national police—picked him up near Saigon and sent him back to the battalion under guard, charged with desertion. Binh could have executed him on the spot, but because the man had not deserted in battle, only in fear of it, he decided instead to make an example of him.

He would administer the punishment himself. But first he approached Ripley. "*Dai-uy* Ripley, *s'il vous plaît*. I request that you go to the command bunker and remain inside. I must give my commander's discipline. You understand. This Marine has brought shame to the Soi Bien. It is correct for my Marines to see this. But I do not wish you to see it."

Ripley complied. *Co-van*s were forbidden to interfere in Vietnamese disciplinary matters. But when the screaming started, he moved to the bunker's entrance and peered out.

The battalion had formed a hollow square around a jeep whose canvas top was down. The deserter, stripped to the waist, was bound to the spare tire mounted on the rear. With a whip fashioned from a piece of heavy-duty communications cable and a wooden tent stake, Binh began laying strokes on the man's back. They formed a crisscross pattern that thickened and deepened until it dissolved into formless gore. The Marine wouldn't stop screaming and Ripley feared that Binh would kill him before he was through. Presently the screams weakened, then ceased. The man's head slumped forward and his knees sagged. Two hospital corpsmen untied him and with his arms slung over their shoulders they half carried him to sick bay, the toes of his jungle boots dragging through the dust.

Eventually the Marine healed and returned to full duty. He never deserted again, and after that punishment neither did any other Third Battalion Marine.

The command group continued to make its way past the deserters. They must be from the Fifty-Sixth ARVN Regiment, Ripley thought. Three battalions from the regiment were deployed in the area, one at Con Thien, another at fire-support base Charlie 3, and the last at Camp Carroll, which lay due west of town on a plateau near Highway 9, in the shadow of Dong Ha Mountain.

Binh was on the radio. When he got off he seemed to have forgotten the deserters. "I have raised the Twentieth Tank Battalion. They received the order to defend Dong Ha with us, and they are moving toward us with the rest of our Marines. We will rendezvous at the west gate of the Dong Ha combat base."

"The Twentieth Tanks—a full battalion. Forty or fifty tanks if most are up and running," Ripley said. "That's a big help. But medium tanks with 90-millimeter main guns aren't going to stop Soviet T-54s. Not in the open, anyway."

"Forty medium tanks are better than ten light antitank weapons," Binh said, smiling.

"Right." Ripley wished he hadn't made such a dumb comment.

The west gate was only a mile outside of town

and they had already walked more than halfway. It took another thirty minutes of pushing through the thickening crowd of refugees to get there.

Lieutenant Colonel Ley, the Vietnamese tank battalion commander, was waiting at the gate for them with his U.S. advisor, an Army major. A long column of new M-48A3 tanks sat in the middle of Highway 9, engines idling, main guns pointing north.

Ley was squat, with a wrestler's build. Despite the mud and the muggy air his boots were as shiny as his new tanks and his uniform looked almost freshly pressed. As he and Binh started their rapid sing-song chatter by the roadside, he kept looking over Binh's shoulder with furtive, darting eyes, as though expecting another, more important person.

The American advisor walked up to Ripley and held out his hand. Muscular and of medium height, he had sandy-haired Midwestern farm boy good looks and a breezy manner.

"Glad you finally got here, Jarhead. Jim Smock. Armor."

"Captain John Ripley. Sure glad to see you and all those ugly machines you're driving, Major."

"What do you mean, ugly? They're beautiful. Now, what the hell's going on? We haven't been getting much word."

Ripley told him about the NVA tanks sighted along Highway 1. Smock grinned and he seemed to grow animated. He swept an arm back toward the column of tanks. "Hell—we can stop them. We've got brand-new tanks and a bunch of tigers who just finished combat training. These guys are real shooters. Trained them myself. Certified combat ready."

He's blowing smoke, thought Ripley. Gunnery training was nothing like trying to hit a tank that could shoot back. And he didn't look ready for combat—no helmet, body armor, or web gear.

"If you just finished training, how'd you wind up here?"

"Lucky, I guess," Smock said. "We were getting ready to move back down south when the Third Division put a hold on us. Told us to stay near Quang Tri, then move up to the Zee with you guys."

Ripley glanced at the two Vietnamese commanders. Binh was talking but he still couldn't get Ley to look him in the eye. The tank battalion commander seemed nervous; he was taking in the scene behind Binh as though looking for a way to end both the conversation and his association with the Marines.

"Your buddy, the light colonel. What's he like?" Ripley said.

Smock laughed shortly. "Bad luck. He acts like we're still back in garrison. Treats these tanks like a fleet of Cadillacs, always trying to keep them ready for inspection. Won't take advice, and won't take chances. Maybe your major can help him strap on a set of balls."

If Binh couldn't, nobody could. "What about the troops?"

"They're green but they'll fight," Smock said, pounding a fist into the palm of his other hand. "We all want to bust some NVA tanks. Firepower. Shock action. The whole nine yards."

He was awfully eager to play swap the bullet. Ripley wondered if he had ever been shot at. Were these tanks really going to be a help?

Nha approached with the handset out. Brigade again.

"Still no confirmed sightings, but the outposts can hear the tanks coming now. A whole bunch. Heavy engine noises, roadwheels squeaking, ground vibrations. They're close. Sounds like they're still in scrub terrain off the roadway, but sooner or later they're going to have to get back on Highway 1 to cross the bridge."

"Don't we have any air up, to tell how many?" Ripley said.

"None yet. Low ceiling."

"C'mon. We must have a thousand feet here."

"Believe me, pal," the Brigade *co-van* said, new tightness in his voice, "we're doing all we can. But big as this is, it ain't the only war in town. Every fire base up here is taking crap and some have already gone under. You're all we have. You've got to hold that goddamn bridge and you've got to do it alone. There's nothing here to back you up with. Do you read me?"

Loud and clear, Ripley thought. What he sensed was true. He should have realized it earlier, without question—the finality of their situation. In a way, this was almost easier than waiting for help that would never come.

"Roger. My show," he said, hoping his voice didn't sound as small and inadequate as he felt.

Soon Brigade came back with another message: They had lost contact with outpost Charlie 1, manned by the Fifty-Seventh ARVN Regiment, the last unit left north of the Cua Viet River. Minutes later, another message: Heavy tanks were reported moving southward between Alpha 2 and Charlie 1. Alpha 2, the northernmost outpost, was overrun. The U.S. naval gunfire spotter there had been killed in action and his radio operator was off the air.

The news hit Ripley hard. He didn't pass it on to Smock right away. "At least we know where the tanks are now," he finally said to the major. "Heading for Charlie 1. Ceiling's still too low to call in air strikes. I'll try Navy guns offshore."

He had planned naval gunfire boxes along with the Brigade advisors and the spot teams from ANGLICO, normally in direct contact with destroyers on the gun line. The boxes were over a half mile wide by more than a mile long and the long axis of each ran east and west, in the direction of fire. Beginning at the north bank of the river, closest to the Dong Ha and French bridges, he had plotted a series of boxes that ran all the way up to the DMZ, generally following the trace of Highway 1.

He keyed his handset to call for two adjacent boxes that covered the ground between Charlie 1 and Alpha 2, where the tanks had last been reported. "Leatherneck, this is Delta. Fire mission. Naval gunfire boxes one-zero-niner and one-one-zero. Tanks and infantry in the open. Cannot observe." On this shoot there was no need to observe or adjust fire. Targets were everywhere. If they missed one they'd hit the one next door.

Brigade rogered his transmission and came right back. "Delta, what's your position? Send it in the clear. No time to unshackle. They can probably see you anyway."

"We're at the back gate," Ripley said.

"Have you linked up?"

"Affirmative."

"Then why aren't you moving back to Dong Ha?"

"Tanks won't budge. We're working on their commanding officer."

"Well, kick his ass. We finally got a spotter plane in the air. They have tanks and armored personnel carriers stretched along Highway 1 all the way back to the DMZ. Must be at least two hundred."

"Jesus! We can't stop that many. We've got to blow that bridge at Dong Ha. Got to buy some time." Ripley tried to keep a pleading tone out of his voice.

"We've been trying to get clearance for the destruct, but can't so far. Those idiots back in Hue and Saigon don't believe the hum we're in. They want to save the bridge for a counterattack."

"What are they smoking back there?" Ripley shouted. "If we try to stop two hundred tanks and God knows how many troops with two rifle companies there's not going to be any goddamned counterattack!"

The voice on the other end sounded weary. "You're right. We can't authorize it, but you've got to blow that bridge. Get moving that way and we'll send some demo up to you. We'll take the heat later."

"Roger, on the way. Out."

Ripley walked back to where Binh and Ley were standing. Binh's neck muscles were tense again and his voice had risen in pitch and volume, berating Ley. Smock tried to intervene but Binh waved him away. Slowly, quietly, Three-Finger Jack positioned himself for an unobstructed view of his commander.

Ripley held up his hand for attention and repeated Brigade's message about the two hundred NVA tanks. Then he took Smock aside and in a voice loud enough for Ley to hear he said, "Tell your colonel that Major Binh and I are going back to Dong Ha and blowing up that bridge, with or without his goddamn precious tanks. There's no other way." Behind him, Binh nodded vigorously. "And warn him that if the enemy gets across the river and his tanks are still here, they'll just be steel tombs."

Ripley nodded to Binh and the two of them turned to go, abruptly. At the head of their small command group they strode back toward Highway 9, leaving the tank battalion commander to face his advisor.

FOUR

*T*hey had nearly reached the highway when Smock came running up behind them. "Wait up! Tanks are on the way!"

Ripley couldn't believe it. "Shit hot, Major. How'd you swing that?"

"I told him I was taking off with you. That did him in. He was ready to cave, after Binh worked him over. He knew if he stayed behind by himself, he'd lose face in front of his troops."

Ripley gestured toward the north bank of the river. "The way they keep bearing down on us over there, he's going to lose face, hat, ass, and poncho if he doesn't watch it."

The ARVN column inched forward until the lead tank was abreast of them. Ley, wearing a helmet with a radio headset and microphone, was riding in the second tank. Smock went and joined him.

"Looks like we get to take the point, *Thieu-ta*," Ripley said to Binh. Binh was cooling down but his face remained hard. He gripped the grunt handles on the lead tank and swung himself up. Ripley, next, reached down to help Nha and Binh's radioman. Last came Three-Finger Jack, catlike, needing no assistance. His half-smile showed the gap in his front teeth and he seemed happy to be moving toward the guns again. Riding shotgun, he made Ripley feel more secure than the entire battalion of tanks.

Ley said something into his mike and the column started forward again, engines rumbling, roadwheels squeaking, treads clacking in slow cadence on the roadway. The humid air began to fill with the smells of fuel and hot grease and exhaust. This time the tanks were moving with the refugees, who still had their eyes on the ground in front of them and were trying to ignore the iron monsters. The men in the lead tank had to warn people continuously to stand clear, creating a bow wave in the tightly packed crowd as the column moved through it. They're gentle with the civilians, Ripley noticed, not like most tankers all full of piss and vinegar.

No more than five minutes later the railroad bridge rose into view. It crossed the Cua Viet almost a mile upstream of the highway bridge at Dong Ha. Ripley pulled out his binoculars for a closer look. The bridge was badly rusted and weeds grew between the track ties like hair out of an old man's ear. One of the southern spans had been destroyed and lay partially submerged in the river. Neither trains nor vehicles could get across. But foot soldiers could, along with their infantry weapons and most of their heavy equipment.

Scanning the far end of the bridge, he saw the NVA battle flag: red over blue, with the yellow star in the center. From the superstructure nearest the north bank, it snapped defiantly in the breeze. "Son of a bitch—they're here!" he said to Binh, who had already spotted the battle flag with his own binoculars.

A handful of North Vietnamese infantrymen were working their way across the bridge and had almost reached the halfway point. They carried K-50 and AK-47 automatic weapons with distinctive banana-shaped magazines, wore mustard-colored khaki uniforms and had helmets with camouflage covers. Their helmet chin straps were tightly buckled, evidence of strict field discipline. The men advanced quickly and methodically, using hand and arm signals instead of shouted commands to leapfrog small fire teams across the bridge. The lead team never moved without a covering team in place.

"Why don't we do something?" Ripley said, desperate. Nobody seemed to hear. Just forward of him, the lead tank's gunner was watching refugees instead of looking northward. Ripley leaned over and slapped the back of the man's helmet to get his attention. The gunner turned around swiftly and glared at him. Ripley drew back as though he himself had been slapped. You weren't ever supposed to touch a Vietnamese on the head, not even pat a small child there. It was a major insult—that was the first thing he'd learned in Vietnam.

"Sorry, Mac. But look!" He jabbed his finger at the bridge. The Vietnamese gunner turned his head reluctantly. The instant he saw the NVA flag and troops he blurted something into his microphone, swung his .50-caliber machine gun around, and opened fire with a long burst.

His tracer rounds ricocheted in lazy, bright-red arcs, a breath before the first pinging sounds of steel on steel returned to the south bank. Seconds later every tank within sight of the bridge was shooting. Streams of tracer fire converged on the target, bouncing off in a crazy-quilt pattern and joining four times as many invisible rounds in a giant buzzing hornet's nest of sound. Fire swept along the bridge and knocked soldiers into the water. Those in the lead squad lay flat, scraping their bellies over the weeds and tracks as they inched toward any skimpy cover they thought they saw.

Then the machine guns on the north bank opened fire in short stuttering bursts and the enemy's tracers, bright green, came vaulting over the river.

Ripley pressed his body hard against the turret and tried to work his way out of the line of fire. Refugees fell to the ground like dominoes in a wave, shrieking and screaming. Once down they grew quiet, letting out only random, tapering wails of terror and pain.

The lead ARVN platoon—the first five tanks in the column—reacted quickly. They trained their 90-millimeter main guns on the bridge and fired their first salvo in unison, with a great roar, sending out a shock wave that knocked Ripley loose from his perch. He had to grab a grunt handle to keep from falling off the tank. Ley's tankers reloaded quickly and fired another salvo. Machine gun fire from the north bank sputtered and died as gun crews left their weapons to escape the next salvo. Troops remaining on the bridge were now on their own. Some still tried, instinctively, to crawl to safety, but there was no real cover and soon all movement stopped.

He almost felt sorry for the poor devils. It was far uglier than watching a man get beaten down in a fistfight, a sight he had always hated. Then he remembered that they would kill him if they had the chance and they would probably have several more before the day was over. What it all came down to was who got whom first.

A final tank salvo carried away the NVA battle flag, bringing a cheer from the defenders of the south bank but no audible reaction from the refugees, who still hugged the earth. Those NVA soldiers who remained began to regroup several hundred yards north of the riverbank, hidden by foliage and a small hill. There were occasional signs of movement but they didn't present enough of a target; ARVN firing grew ragged, then stopped.

The refugees started to get up and collect their belongings. Smock's upper body emerged from the commander's hatch of the next tank in line. He removed his helmet, tucked it under his arm, and flashed Ripley a wolfish grin and thumbs-up sign. Looks like he just scored the winning touchdown, Ripley thought. This time, anyway.

The fight had slowed their advance by fifteen or twenty minutes. It was almost nine. They had to push on and get to the bridge. The column moved forward again, threading its way through the thickening crowd of civilians. Approaching Dong Ha, they saw new signs of the destructive power of the enemy's heavy artillery. Corpses lay dismembered and forgotten along the roadside. Dead livestock looked like full-blown bagpipes with bloated bellies and stiff legs sticking out at crazy angles. Carts were overturned, their contents—clothing, utensils, furniture—strewn in all directions. There was no looting.

Here and there the stream of refugees parted where small family groups stood, islands huddled around recent victims of the shelling. When nothing more could be done, when the last writhing of a dying body ceased, an island would dissolve like so many clods of earth being washed away.

Ripley spoke to Binh for the first time since the action at the railroad bridge. "Let's see if we still have some ships on the gun line. Let them earn their

pay. They can take out some of those artillery positions. Nha?" Nha handed him the radio handset. "Leatherneck, this is Delta. Fire mission: Boxes Alpha Tango one-zero-five, one-zero-six . . ."

The response from naval guns was prompt. Moments later high-velocity rounds were tearing overhead, ripping the sky apart as though it were a giant piece of canvas. They continued for ten minutes, then stopped abruptly. Except for the low rumbling of tanks at near-idling speed, the sounds of battle had evaporated, and for the first time in days silence fell thick and sweet around them.

"All day, all night, all weather, all right! We sure shook up those NVA cannon-cockers, didn't we, Nha?" Ripley said, nodding his head vigorously. Nha, uncomprehending, nodded back, mirroring his *co-van*'s excitement. Three-Finger Jack looked on with detached amusement.

They were within a few hundred yards of Dong Ha when the lull ended. At first there was no sound, only orange flashes and black cottonballs of smoke that blossomed simultaneously all over town. Then came the noise, loud and rolling, of countless guns firing together and shells exploding as if hundreds of trees, lightning-struck, were cracking and splitting and the sound was reverberating off the walls of a giant canyon.

Binh and Ripley stared at each other. Over the din, cupping his hands around his mouth, Ripley screamed, "A time-on-target! That's why they weren't firing. They were just setting up for this." The roaring and the pounding were inside his head pushing outward and he felt it would burst, spewing out his confused thoughts. He wondered how many guns there were, hundreds maybe, and how many civilians in Dong Ha, all the ones who lived there and the thousands passing through. He wondered where their tank column would have been if the firefight at the railroad bridge hadn't held them up, and why the enemy was going after the town instead of the ARVN tanks or at least the Marines dug in along the riverbank. And then he wondered how long it would be before the NVA gunners got tired of making rubble bounce in the town and started walking their fire westward.

Everything had come to a halt along the highway. It made no sense anymore for the tank column to try and push through, even if it could. The refugees had stopped on the outskirts of town and tried to back away from the artillery barrage until the press of oncoming bodies packed the road solid. If the artillery fire shifted westward, no one would escape.

But the fire didn't shift. It settled into a continuous pattern of twelve-round salvos that swept back and forth, from one side of Dong Ha to the other. Gradually the black smoke drifted up and formed a thick gray roof over the town. Fires burned everywhere.

Who could possibly be left alive in there? Ripley thought. Then it occurred to him that Ley might have helped save their lives by wasting more precious minutes trying to protect his tanks. Whatever the reason, they couldn't stay in place or they would die.

Ripley tapped Binh on the shoulder. "We've got to turn around. I know another way to get to the highway bridge."

"What is that?" Binh asked, unfamiliar with the area.

"Another road runs from the west gate—where we rendezvoused with Twentieth Tanks—along the southwestern perimeter of the combat base. I used it five years ago. It intersects with Highway 1 about a mile south of Dong Ha. We can move north to the bridge from there. It's longer, but we'll never get through this way and we can't just sit here trapped, waiting for the enemy to shift fire onto us."

Binh rubbed his chin in deep thought. A minute later he said, "*Dai-uy*, I have good idea. We will take the west gate road."

Ripley didn't remind Binh that the idea had come from him. It was always like this—Binh taking the best of his advice after convincing himself that the American's suggestions were a reflection of his own thinking. That was all right with Ripley. The behavior was part of an unspoken code that the *co-van*s had to learn to decrypt. The code covered bad suggestions too. When Ripley's advice was not appreciated, Binh wouldn't allow his counterpart to lose face by contradicting him. He would just let the matter drop.

"But first we must convince Colonel Ley to move the tanks," Binh said.

They walked back to the second tank and yelled

up to Smock to get the tank battalion commander, still buttoned up inside. Smock pounded on the turret hatch with the butt of his pistol until the hatch opened slowly, cautiously, and Ley's head emerged. He scanned the horizon nervously, without looking at Smock or Binh.

Let's see how much English he understands, Ripley said to himself. He cupped his hands around his mouth to be sure Ley could hear him from the ground. "We've got to turn around and get out of here. We can take the old west gate road to get to the bridge. I'll lead the way and show you where it is."

Ley didn't appear to understand, but after a moment he said something in Smock's ear. "The answer's no," Smock yelled back. "If we attract attention to ourselves by moving away from this shield of refugees, the enemy will shift fire onto us."

Ripley cursed. "Why is the enemy going to treat these refugees any better than the ones in town, especially when the target includes a stalled tank column?"

"I know," Smock said. "Let me talk to him." He tapped Ley on the shoulder and said a few more words to him. Ley nodded, eyes making one more sweep of the horizon, then disappeared down the hatch. "It's okay," Smock said. "He'll give the order to turn around. He's so shook up by this artillery he'll agree to anything."

Ripley and Binh climbed back on their tank. Marine riflemen cleared a path through the crowd. Rather than reverse the order of march by having each tank spin 180 degrees on its tracks, Binh and Ripley started a second column running alongside the first in the opposite direction, heading back to the west gate.

Agitated chattering preceded the lead tank as refugees realized it was turning around. Tanks following in trace had to keep the column closed up to prevent civilians from flowing like water into the gaps, where they might be crushed. As the tank column doubled in width, the crowd's density increased.

This is taking forever, Ripley thought. The enemy must see what we're doing. But no attack yet. Maybe they really don't know we're here. Maybe their commander at the railroad bridge is reluctant to tell his seniors that he got his butt kicked.

He had to report the change in plans to Brigade, which was unhappy about the delay but understood the reason for it. Before he signed off, Brigade had a message for him.

"Hey, Delta—remember a song that starts, 'From the halls of Montezuma'?"

"Of course. Why? Over."

"Start humming. Out."

The Marines' Hymn. What did that mean? Were U.S. Marines coming to the rescue? The Special Landing Force, maybe? That would be up to two thousand more troops, a lot of extra firepower, forward air controllers to call in the fast burners, helicopters and amtracks for mobility . . . He tried not to get his hopes up. He had to be stoic, live in the present and work with what there was in front of him, not chase after pipe dreams. What were the chances of reinforcements arriving in time to help with the bridge? What were the chances that he would even get to the bridge in time?

His tank finally cleared the west gate and picked up speed gradually on the less-traveled perimeter road, careful not to run away from the rest of the column, still mired in the crowd. He wondered why refugees weren't following the tanks. This road was a quicker way—the only way right now—to Highway 1 and it would take them farther south, farther from the enemy. They probably think our tanks are the enemy's only remaining target, he decided. As more tanks reached the perimeter road, the column's speed built up. Everyone expected incoming artillery to pursue them along the new route any minute. But the guns were still pounding what was left of Dong Ha.

The perimeter road rose gently before it turned east to Highway 1 and as they neared the crest of the slope Ripley looked back. Beyond the tank column lay the Cua Viet River and the damaged railroad bridge. Farther east past the combat base and its low-lying buildings was Dong Ha, the only sign of civilization, or what used to be civilization, in the barren landscape. From this distance the artillery bombardment sounded less threatening, mere thunder in the far reaches of the overcast sky. Across the river from Dong Ha he could see the ribbon of Highway 1. Using his binoculars he began to search along this northern stretch for NVA tanks and armored personnel carriers. If they were trying to make good time, they would probably still be roadbound.

He saw their tanks almost immediately, kicking up rooster tails of sand and mud as they raced toward the bridge. His stomach jumped, the same funny feeling he had in a fast-moving elevator. He got Binh's attention and pointed at them. "There they are, *Thieu-ta*, T-54s!" he shouted. "God, they're ugly!" They were green like the body bags in the morgue, and on their little bubble-shaped turrets they carried big red stars. They had extra-long 100-millimeter main guns and expeditionary gas drums lashed in back, and they were rolling with hatches open. Confident, he thought. Through his binoculars he could see the helmeted heads of drivers and gunners leaning forward in anticipation of their victory roll into a town full of dead civilians. They might have been a pack of wild and hungry jackals loping across the plain toward a lone, rotting carcass in the distance.

Ripley got his driver's attention and pumped his right fist up and down several times. Speed it up, mate, he said silently. It's time to get back in the war.

FIVE

*S*mock must see them too, he thought. Smock's tank moved out of the column with two others and into firing positions at the side of the road. The NVA column had just passed a sharp bend in Highway 1 that took it southeastward for a short distance before turning south again toward Dong Ha. During this jag, its right flank was exposed to Smock's tanks.

They trained their 90-millimeter main guns on the first three NVA tanks and fired simultaneously, with a giant, shattering crack. The three high-velocity rounds were marked by bright-red tracers and through his binoculars Ripley watched them slice over the abandoned combat base and across the river. The lead tank shuddered for a moment, absorbing a hit, then disintegrated, hurling chunks of metal, jagged pieces of tread and flaming expeditionary cans through the air. He shifted his binoculars to the second. Its turret had been swept away and flames darted from a hole in the top of its chassis. The last one was smothered in fire.

Smock's tanks reloaded and took on the next three T-54s, which had been slowed by the devastation in front of them. Each ARVN tank fired separately this time, and each again found its target. The muffled thump of explosions drifted across the river and continued in an irregular pattern as flames reached stowed ammunition.

The enemy column dissolved. Tanks broke out of it and swirled in all directions, trying to find their assailants while buttoned up.

"Burn, you miserable bastards," Ripley said. "We'll beat you to the bridge yet."

Then Smock led the three ARVN tanks back into the column and it began to move again, over the crest of the hill. This victory in the battalion's first tank-on-tank engagement seemed to pump new life into the South Vietnamese. Smock was grinning again, but now Ripley was the one to give a thumbs-up sign. Ley was nowhere in sight.

Half an hour later, they were nearing the intersection of the perimeter road and Highway 1. His radio had been silent since the Montezuma message but fragmentary reports of fighting continued to arrive on Binh's tactical nets, plugged into Vietnamese Marine and ARVN chains of command. Binh seemed to be calm as he translated the reports for Ripley, though the radio chatter sounded intermittently high-pitched and excited.

"South Vietnamese units are falling back across the river," Binh said. "Some ARVN soldiers are throwing away their weapons and helmets."

"Helmets! With all this incoming? They've got to be crazy to do that."

Presently they reached the intersection with Highway 1 and he could see them, a second wave of deserters who had removed badges and insignia to blend in with the refugees. They must be from the Fifty-Seventh Regiment, he thought. The ones from the Fifty-Sixth couldn't have made it through Dong Ha during the last attack. These men looked scared but not terrorized. Unlike the civilians, they knew where they were heading. And they were going to survive no matter what. They'd worry about the rest later, after better men had died to protect them.

Binh's radio continued to pour out bad news. "Tanks are crossing the Dong Ha bridge unopposed," he said to Ripley, speaking as he listened. "They are being followed closely by NVA infantry units . . . The enemy is in Dong Ha . . . Dong Ha has fallen." Binh took the radio handset and held it at arm's length as though he wanted to choke the life out of it. He cursed it in Vietnamese.

Ripley wondered who was spreading the stories. According to their own battalion tactical net, the two companies along the Cua Viet were beginning to duel with enemy troops across the river, but none had attempted to cross the bridge yet. If enough people believed the rumors and a general panic broke out it would be much harder to hold on to the town. And the Third ARVN Division would never be able to regroup down south unless Dong Ha held out awhile. He wondered about the effect on Soi Bien morale of ARVN deserters passing through their lines alongside the refugees.

Binh had fallen silent. His mouth was clamped shut and the hollows under his cheekbones seemed to be caving in. When he spoke his voice was tense, as though a razor had shredded his words. "*Dai-uy* Ripley, *s'il vous plaît*, I am going to send a message on my command radio. I want you to send the same message on your advisor radio. There must be no misunderstanding. This is the message: 'Ignore all rumors that Dong Ha has fallen. There are Vietnamese Marines in Dong Ha. We will fight in Dong Ha. We will die in Dong Ha. We will not leave. As long as one Marine draws a breath of life, Dong Ha will belong to us.'"

While this message was being transmitted up and down the chains of command, the ARVN tank column continued to push north along Highway 1. The scene was far worse than the one on Highway 9.

Bodies and burning wreckage cluttered the road and its shoulders. Here there were no more signs of stoic perseverance; refugees were running and stumbling, leaving children and elders behind. The whites of their eyes revealed new terror that went beyond a state of mind. It was physical, like a huge boulder blocking their way, and unless they ran at it and pushed it aside it would destroy them. Action was the only antidote to the paralysis of dread.

The tank column continued to move slowly through the stream of refugees, past a community burial ground. High-explosive shells had ripped into it, opening graves and flinging gravestones around as if they were no heavier than a fistful of poker chips. Even the spirits are uprooted, Ripley thought. The desecration is complete.

Deserters from the Fifty-Seventh Regiment were still passing by. Suddenly, without warning to Ripley, Binh leapt off the top of the tank and landed in front of one of them. Three-Finger Jack followed and took up a protective position nearby, holding his carbine at the ready. Binh seized the soldier by the shirt and yanked him from side to side. The man went limp, his arms dangling and flopping like a rag doll's.

"*Linh di dau do*?" Binh screamed. Where do you think you're going, soldier? The man mumbled back, his jaw barely moving. Binh switched into English so Ripley would understand. "My Marines will not die for you to live!" he said, and pushed the deserter away. The man staggered but stayed on his feet, swaying, head and shoulders slumped.

Binh drew his .45-caliber pistol from its holster. Refugees moving south veered away from the pair but paid them no more attention. He pulled back on the sidearm's slide and eased it forward, chambering a round. Then he released the safety and held the muzzle against the deserter's forehead. The man still made no effort to resist.

Binh pulled the trigger and the recoil jerked his arm back. The force of the shot slammed the deserter into the side of Binh's tank. He stood there briefly, a neat purple hole in his forehead where the bullet had entered; then he pitched forward and collapsed in the roadway. The back of his head was a messy pulp of blood and brains.

God in heaven! Ripley thought. Southerners killing Southerners. What's happening to them? What's happening to all of us?

Binh stood over the fallen deserter and held his pistol at the ready, muzzle pointing skyward. Three-Finger Jack had his carbine in his shoulder now, prepared to fire on anyone who threatened Binh. He was alert as a panther crouched for the kill.

The warning didn't count for much. Deserters continued to move south with the refugees, swinging wide as they passed Binh and the pool of blood spreading at his feet. They couldn't be shamed into fighting and they couldn't be scared into it. They were beyond caring, shuffling past the body of their comrade.

For a moment Binh looked confused, defeated. Jack lowered his weapon and approached his com-

mander. He whispered in Binh's ear, careful not to address him face to face, which would have been a sign of disrespect. He had never approached his *thieu-ta* without being summoned, nor spoken to him first.

Not looking at Jack, Binh nodded and holstered his pistol. The two of them returned to the lead tank and climbed back on, leaving the deserter where he had fallen. Like a dead dog in the road, Ripley thought. He didn't say a word to Binh.

Binh gave the signal to move out and soon the tanks were pressing against the tide again. The lead tank inched forward, gently forcing refugees aside. The heavy shelling of Dong Ha had finally stopped; now only occasional harassing rounds landed along Highway 1, enough to keep fear alive in the crowd, whose density finally brought the column to a halt.

Smock dismounted and walked up to the lead tank. After Ripley climbed down, he spoke to him privately. "That candy-ass Ley doesn't want to take his precious tanks any farther."

"But we have a good half mile to go," Ripley said.

"He says he's been getting reports on the radio that the bridge has been destroyed by tank and artillery fire."

"A hundred tanks could fire for three days and still not knock that monster down. And why would the NVA want to take out a bridge they're trying to cross?"

"He doesn't want to move the tanks all the way up to the forward slope of the ridge that overlooks the river. He thinks they'll do just as well back here in defilade."

"Goddamn it!" Ripley said, slamming his hand on the side of the tank. "Can't he see what's happening? The world is coming apart right in front of our eyes, and we're the only ones with a chance of holding it together."

"Relax, will you? I've already told him we need to push the tanks into what's left of those dogpatch huts along the south bank. We can get some concealment and some outstanding firing positions. Not much cover, but if we shoot first it won't matter. We got six kills from nearly maximum range and they never knew what hit them."

"Maybe Binh can convince him."

"I don't know," Smock said, lowering his voice. He lit a new cigarette from the glowing butt of an old one. "Ley's getting shakier by the minute. And after seeing Binh blow that deserter away, he's more afraid of him than the enemy. He's really gone into hiding. Doesn't even respond when I talk to him. I think he's lost it. Look at the way his mouth hangs open."

"Well I'm not waiting for him to grow a set of stones before I take down that bridge," Ripley said. "We're too close now. Stay and breast-feed him if you want. I'm walking." He signaled to Nha and elbowed his way through the crowd, past the lead tank. Jack glanced at Binh, who didn't move with the *co-van* this time.

Ley approached the two advisors, then stopped and hung back. Smock ran over to him and grabbed the front of his unbuttoned flak jacket. He started shouting something that Ripley couldn't make out; when he finished he shouted orders to the first two tank commanders and remounted the second tank. He's done it, Ripley thought. Squeezed a light section of tanks out of Ley. Ripley and Nha pushed their way back through the refugees toward the lead tank. Binh actually smiled when he was told what had happened.

The tanks resumed their slow roll. Within minutes they were passing the trailing edge of the mob, people who had just made it through town before the heavy shelling started. It was like moving through a rain squall: one minute you couldn't see two feet in front of you, the next minute the air was clear and you could see for miles. Now the tanks picked up speed, careening around corpses and burning vehicles. Artillery fire intensified as they neared the center of Dong Ha but they pushed through, the men hugging their turrets, trying to make themselves as small as possible. It seemed only minutes before they were there, behind the small ridge overlooking the Cua Viet at the intersection of Highways 1 and 9, a place called the Triangle.

Ripley and Smock dismounted, trailed by Nha, and walked to the crest for their first good look at the bridge they'd be trying to take down.

Smock whistled through his teeth. "Jesus—it's huge!"

"I rode over this sonofabitch five years ago, right after the SeaBees built it. Didn't seem so big back then," Ripley said. "When they build a bridge to hold tanks, they don't screw around."

The south end of the bridge was barely a hundred yards away, down a slight slope. The hillside lay exposed to observation and direct fire from the north bank. Along the riverbank Binh's Marines, the Soi Bien, manned their fighting holes. Halfway down the slope a Dye Marker bunker, left over from a high-tech DMZ barrier project abandoned years before, offered a safety island of sorts. Should have called it Die Marker, Ripley thought. The project had killed a lot of good Marines. Now maybe it could save a life or two.

He scanned the area through his binoculars. "Looks like a hundred-yard dash, twelve seconds or more, broken into two parts. Think they can find us in twelve seconds?" he asked Smock. The question was rhetorical. He knew they could, even their worst shooters.

As Ripley was scanning the riverbank, a Vietnamese Marine in tiger suit and helmet climbed out of his fighting hole and began to crawl toward the south end of the bridge. He had two light antitank weapons slung across his shoulders, M-72 LAAWs, and he was dragging an unpainted ammo box with each hand. Ripley refocused his binoculars. It was the Second Company's rocket squad leader, a sergeant. He wondered what the ammo was for and, looking more closely, saw that the boxes didn't have lids and were full of dirt, not ammo. The sergeant was dragging a portable foxhole with him. He reached the bridge at the point where it joined the south ramp. The middle of the structure had a slight arch, higher than either riverbank, that would mask him from the enemy. He stacked the two boxes and began to prepare his LAAWs for firing. He extended the throwaway tube on one, checking it carefully. Satisfied, he set it down and extended the tube on the second one. Then he took up a prone firing position and sighted carefully along the bridge, settling down to wait for the first T-54.

"Get serious," Smock said. "He's going after T-54s with a piss-ant LAAW?"

"More guts than brains," said Ripley. "That first tank'll barrel across the bridge and crush him before he can get one round off."

The lead T-54 clacked up the concrete ramp on the bridge's north end. It showed a lot of hard use. Mud caked the treads and large roadwheels and clumps of brush snagged in off-road maneuvering stuck to the sides. The hatch on the bubble turret was still closed, limiting the commander's view.

The next tank remained well back, at least a hundred yards. No walking infantry were in sight and it didn't look as though any NVA troops were positioned to provide close-in protection, axiomatic for tank-infantry operations.

The lead tank stopped just short of the bridge, turret rotating slowly, letting the main gun traverse the front, then inched forward and stopped again. The suspension system rocked it gently into a level position and the main gun began another leisurely swing.

Smock was shaking his head. "Where's their outside set of eyeballs?" he said. "It's crazy to ride blind like that. But since they're out there in the open anyway, why don't they charge over the bridge instead of hanging back?"

The sergeant saw or felt the tank coming and drew his knees forward, raising his body for a better position. When he fired the LAAW there was a loud noise but not much visible back blast. The round sailed over the T-54 and detonated on the north bank, short of the second tank.

"Bad angle. Still too low," said Ripley.

The tank's main gun pointed downstream. The commander hadn't seen the LAAW fired, and evidently nobody had told him about it on the radio.

The sergeant raised himself above his thin dirt shield. He took careful aim and fired the second LAAW. Almost instantaneously, the round detonated where the tank's chassis and turret met. The main gun started swinging back toward the bridge but jammed after moving less than a foot. The turret motor raced and whined.

Finally, the tank commander lifted his hatch and peered out. Smoke poured from the turret. The sergeant stayed close to the ground, behind his ammo boxes. For several seconds nothing happened.

Then the tank commander backed his machine off the bridge and settled into position upstream. Rotating the tank on its treads, he pointed his main gun toward the south end of the bridge. Smoke rising through the turret petered out as the crew brought the fire inside under control. Meanwhile, tanks next in line pulled back and sought cover, keeping their main guns trained on the bridge.

"Can you believe that, Major?" Ripley said. "Those sorry bastards make Ley look like a man-eating tiger."

"I hope they keep it up. They don't look like real tankers to me."

"Ready to make a run for the Dye Marker?"

"I don't know. Are we going to zigzag or beeline it?" Smock looked uncomfortable.

"Straight line all the way. Get there before the bullets do. You've got to keep up with the grunts now."

"What about your radioman?" Nha, as always, was nearby. He crouched forward with a tight grip on the handset, ready to run.

"He's pretty quick, even with the radio. But he's not going beyond the Dye Marker bunker."

"How come?"

"He's our only contact with Brigade, and he can see everything there is to report from there. Besides, I need a witness."

"A witness?"

"If we get blown away I want someone alive to tell the story."

Smock looked him squarely in the eye. "You scare me, Captain," he said.

"Hell, I've been scared all along," Ripley said.

It was time.

SIX

*T*he three of them broke into the open, heading for the Dye Marker bunker. Nha's radio antenna whipped crazily. For several seconds no one fired. They were halfway there before they heard the crack of the first shots over their own heavy breathing. The shooting was ragged and probably wild.

The Marines dug into the bank were unaware of runners moving down the slopes behind them. They returned fire, and the firing from both banks was heavy by the time Ripley and the others reached the bunker. Accustomed to moving together in combat, he and Nha dove for cover simultaneously, as though they'd choreographed it. Smock flopped behind the bunker a second later.

By now the shots were accurate. They thudded into the sandbags piled around the bunker; sand trickled from dozens of newly opened wounds. The three men crawled along the sheltered side of the bunker until they reached a place where they could crouch. Nha had the radio handset at his ear again, serious, sad-eyed. Old Sobersides doesn't want to miss a thing, Ripley thought.

"Piss-poor way to make a living, Jarhead," Smock said. "Give me my tanks any day. Nothing like a nice smooth ride behind some heavy armor."

"I saw those tin boxes you busted open back there. Poor bastards inside didn't have a chance." Ripley would never trade places with a tanker.

Looking toward the south bank, he caught the eye of a Marine in his fighting hole, a squad leader from Second Company. Maybe he could get that squad to cover them by fire when they made their dash for the bridge.

Ripley waved. He pointed to himself and to the bridge. He pumped his right arm up and down, the signal for running at double time. Then he pointed to the squad leader and held up his carbine and pretended to shoot at the north bank.

The squad leader recognized him and flashed a big toothy grin. "*Gia phai!*" Okay!

It was a good thing he'd taken time to talk with these riflemen instead of hanging around the battalion command group all the time. The Soi Bien knew him, trusted him. They'd help him out right away, not wait for orders to filter down the chain of command. Maybe he'd get there yet.

Now he had to wait for the NVA to stop firing. They had to get tired of beating up those sandbags. But there was no time. They might rush the bridge any minute.

Hurry up, you bastards, stop shooting! he thought.

Several minutes later the tempo slowed, settling into ragged exchanges of rifle and machine gun fire. "Ready, Major?" he said to Smock.

"You bet."

Smock's eyes were fixed on the north side of the bridge. He was scared too. He knew the NVA was waiting for them. At least they had covering fire now, enough to screw up the NVA's aim. If everything went right the enemy wouldn't get a clear shot.

Ripley looked back at the south bank and held his hand in the air, making sure he had the squad leader's attention. The Vietnamese proceeded to give preparatory commands to his men. He went right by the book, as though he were back on the rifle range. Ripley followed him silently, translating. Unlock . . . Aim in . . . Then he brought his hand down in a short chopping motion.

"*Ban!*" the leader called, giving the command to fire.

One of the squad's automatic weapons stuttered in two- and three-round bursts, quickly joined by another upstream. Rifle shots built up rapidly around the automatic weapons. Within seconds the Soi Bien had a steady base of fire hitting NVA positions on the north bank. Anyone brave or dumb enough to expose himself aiming a return shot would become an immediate target.

Ripley and Smock broke from cover and ran straight for the bridge, leaving Nha behind. Once again the north bank was slow to react, giving them those few extra seconds to run the distance.

Ripley's canteens knocked against his butt. His holster slapped his thigh and his helmet slid over his head, covering his eyes. He felt like a Keystone Cop running in slow motion. As he neared the bridge geysers of dirt began to kick up in front of him, and the first sound of firing came from the north bank. It was weak, spasmodic, compared with the steady base of Marine fire. Then through the rattle of small arms came a new noise, louder and deeper. Fire from a heavy machine gun. It sounded like a 12.7-millimeter, the same type that had twice shot down his helo at Khe Sanh. This one must be mounted on a tank, he thought.

He willed himself forward, driving harder and harder with each stride and thinking that any minute his legs might collapse. He was almost there. When he reached the base of an earthen berm he dove into the ground, skidding through mud and sand and pebbles. There he lay for a moment, sides heaving.

Firing from the north bank slowed, then stopped. Bastards can't see us anymore, he thought. We must be in defilade. Where was Smock? "Major!" He raised his head to look and it made him dizzy, the way he'd felt with bed spins after drinking cheap booze. He lowered his head. Settle down, he said to himself. Breathe deep, slow. But where was Smock? He couldn't make it without Smock. Then he raised his head again and there was the major, panting and grinning.

"You okay, Ripley? Looks like you lost it for a while."

"Got carried away outrunning bullets."

"Don't seize up on me now. You have to figure out how to blow this bridge. I can help, but I don't know squat about demo."

"Stick with me, Major. If Brigade sent us anything to work with up here, we'll do it right by the numbers."

"Just don't pass out on me, that's all."

He'd never been dizzy like this. Not boxing, not in Ranger or commando training. He was running on adrenaline by now. God, how long could that last? How much longer would he have to keep going?

He looked around for the demo, wondering if they'd busted their butts for nothing. About twenty yards away five ARVN soldiers huddled against the berm. Half stacked, half scattered around them were a dozen or more unpainted pine boxes and at least as many canvas haversacks with long carrying straps. The soldiers stared ahead with wide, blank eyes.

They were wearing sateen field uniforms instead of camouflage jungle suits—probably garrison troops. Maybe they were from an engineer outfit in the rear. But even if they knew something about demo they wouldn't be any help. They were paralyzed. The firing must have built up just after they'd hauled all the gear down the hill.

He moved closer. The boxes were about a foot high, a foot wide, three feet long. They looked like artillery ammo boxes. He read the stencil on the closest one:

> DEMOLITION
> TNT, 1/2 LB BLOCKS
> WT 75
> CU 3.0
> LOADED 9−69

The soldiers had already ripped the tops off the boxes, exposing grainy gray blocks of TNT inside. They looked like large cakes of industrial soap, but if one of those cakes was detonated close enough it would make a man bleed from the ears. With 150 to a box, they'd get some big bangs. Smock was shaking his head, smiling, as if to say they had enough demo to blow up Asia. Ripley just hoped they had enough for the bridge. There's so much steel in the underside of this monster the SeaBees could have built a goddamn battleship, he thought.

The stringers—the bridge's longitudinal strength members—were constructed of steel I-beam girders. There were six of them, about three feet between each. The girders had vertical straps thirty to thirty-six inches high and flanges that extended three to four inches on either side of the straps.

On top of the stringers lay steel deck plates of indeterminate size, probably too thick to cut. Bridging timbers sat on the plates, perpendicular to the stringers. Not needed for strength, they were used simply as dunnage to keep tanks and other tracked vehicles from tearing up the bridge. Two more sets of timbers ran lengthwise down each side of the bridge, serving as curbs for vehicles when rainfall made things slippery. The timbers looked about two feet thick.

The bridge was supported by five massive, steel-reinforced concrete piers. They rose twenty to thirty feet out of the river and were as wide as the bridge itself, close to twenty feet. In thickness, they ran between five and six. It would be useless to try and knock one down.

So there it was. Two to four feet of wood on top of God only knew how much steel . . . on top of six sets of stringers . . . on top of a set of monster piers . . .

"You could pound this bastard all day with artillery and air strikes and still not knock it down," he said to Smock. "Hell, it would be easier to divert the river through Hanoi than destroy this bloody bridge."

Smock looked at Ripley as though he had been betrayed. "Then what the hell are we doing up here, for Chrissakes?"

"Destroying this bloody bridge," Ripley said grimly. "Who said it had to be easy, huh?"

He wondered if he should set the timbers on fire, then decided that would be too hard. And after the fire burned itself out the steel would still be there. It would have to be the stringers. He would have to cut every last one of them, all at the exact same time. Just as he'd been taught at Ranger school.

There, under the tall Georgia pines at Fort Benning, the demolitions instructor had given due credit to the railroad men who used earmuff charges to cut track. "Someday you might have to cut track," he said. "But not to build a railroad. You might have to keep somebody else's railroad from running on time. And you'll have to do it quickly and cleanly and not use a whole lot more demo than you need. Doesn't take much, if you do it right. Think of putting on a pair of earmuffs, crooked. One earmuff covers the front part of your left ear and the other covers the back part of your right ear. If you put the earmuffs on straight—that is, if you place the charges on exactly opposite sides of the rail—the two explosions cancel each other out, even though they put a terrible squeeze on that poor piece of rail.

"But if you offset the charges like this, like the crooked earmuffs, the moments of force of the two charges will push right past each other and shear the rail cleanly. The old railroad men called this a twister. The Brits used twisters to cut track on the River Kwai bridge. In the book, not the movie. They were backups for the main charge, set with electrical detonators to cut the bridge supports.

"You always need a backup system. Charges fail . . . Fuzes fail . . . Detonators fail . . ."

Detonators. Someone must have sent them up with all the demo. Where were they? Maybe the ARVNs dropped them on their way down the hill. He looked around for the engineers. They were gone, melted away, had probably taken off along the riverbank downstream. Out of the war.

He cursed. Now he'd never find the detonators. There was no time to look for them, and if they didn't show up he'd have to try the hand grenade trick, unscrewing the cap and fuze. That would only give him four seconds to clear out. If he were working under the bridge it would mean dropping into the river from a height of three stories, and with a load of gear on his back. If he didn't bust his ass in the fall he'd sink like a stone. And if he didn't sink, the bridge would fall on top of him or the NVA would pick him off while he fought to stay afloat. The hand grenade trick. Some field expedient, he thought.

He had to figure out where to make the cut. It couldn't be too close to the south bank; the cut span might drop on dry land and then the enemy would be able to get across. He decided to make it well over the water, a hundred feet out, by the first pier. He would put earmuffs on each girder and run the charges on a diagonal so the torque from the explosion would twist the span right off its foundations, in this case the abutment and the first pier. The entire span would drop into the river. There was no way the enemy could get his tanks across a hundred-foot gap.

Smock stared up at the bridge like a farm boy seeing his first skyscraper. He was beginning to appreciate the problem.

"I think we've lucked out," Ripley said. "Each channel between the stringers looks wide enough to hold a box of TNT. We can load boxes into the channels sideways and I can drag them out over the water. I'll start in the downstream channel and take the first box out to the first pier. Then I'll position the rest of the boxes in the other channels along a diagonal that runs back toward this shoreline. I can use the satchel charges—in those haversacks—to set up twisters on each girder. They'll cut the I-beams and detonate the TNT, which'll torque the near span right into the drink."

"I don't know what in hell you're talking about," Smock said, "but I trust you. What should I do?"

"Once I get out there you can help load demo boxes into the channels. Two boxes and two satchel charges for each channel. And while I'm getting started, you can hunt for a box or two of detonators—blasting caps—to set the bridge off. They should be in a small wooden box with a hinged cover. Each detonator has its own recess in the box, just like bits for a drill. We've got to find those miserable blasting caps. Otherwise, lighting this thing may be the last thing I ever do."

"What's in the satchel charge?"

"Composition C-4. Soft plastic explosive. You can mold it around things for special cutting jobs. Even take down a tree with it." He picked up a haversack and looked inside. The explosive was a creamy off-white, the color and texture of vanilla fudge. A C-4 fudge feast. He remembered how hungry he was.

His old company gunnery sergeant had used composition C-4 to heat his "dynamite coffee." A small pinch of the stuff made a hot fire and while it was burning the gunny didn't have to worry about anybody hanging around to share his cup. There hadn't really been anything to fear. Plastic C-4 would burn but it wouldn't explode without primer cord.

"Oh. I almost forgot," he said to Smock. "While you're searching for the detonators keep your eyes open for a coil of fuze cord, primer cord. You'll know it when you see it."

"I will, huh?"

"But first I'll need some help getting through that wire."

To prevent sabotage to the undersection of the bridge the SeaBees had rigged a six-foot chain-link fence on the river side of the abutment. A Y-shaped yoke at the top of the fence held three rolls of concertina wire, which were partially extended in springy semi-coils. The concertina pressed against the bottom of the stringers, leaving no clear access to the bridge's underside without extensive wire cutting. The old type of concertina was studded with thousands of steel barbs to puncture and tear anyone trying to work through it. But this new type, German steel tape, was worse. Small, razor-sharp blades of metal would slash a person foolhardy enough to take it on. Death by a thousand cuts, the ancient Chinese torture.

The SeaBees had thought of everything. Hell, he'd bleed to death by the time he got out to the first pier. At least they hadn't stuffed the wire all the way into the channels. Once he made it through the top of the fence, he might be okay. Until it was time to come back in, anyway.

He took off his helmet and slung his carbine diagonally across his back. Then he picked up two satchel charges and swung one over each shoulder. "I'm going through that razor wire," he said. "I need you up on the fence with me to pull the concertina as far down into the yoke as possible, so I can kick my way through. Then I want you to load the demo into each channel as I come back for it, so I don't have to go through that wire every time."

"Wire looks plenty mean, Rip."

"We won't know how mean until I get going. Same for the demo boxes fitting into the channel. We won't really know until we give it a bloody go. And it will be bloody. For both of us."

He began to climb the fence, where it rose to the stringer farthest downstream.

*T*he down-
stream side of the bridge was relatively quiet. Most
of the infantrymen on both banks had dug in upstream where the road ran up to the bridge, the
foliage was thinner, and fields of fire were better.
The flurry of shooting that started during the final
dash to the bridge had settled into a measured, delib-
erate duel across the water. Single rifle shots and
short bursts from machine guns sounded in random
sequence as the men took more careful aim, conserv-

ing their ammunition. Behind the staccato of small-arms fire rolled the distant rumble of artillery searching ceaselessly along Highways 9 and 1 for more victims.

It was almost peaceful as he began to climb the chain-link fence. A deceptive peace. There had to be thousands of NVA troops stacked up on the north bank by now. Against a couple hundred Marines, at most. The fragment of an old ditty stuck in his head: "Ten thousand gobs laid down their swabs / To fight one sick Marine."

He got to the yoke at the top of the fence and reached up and back to grasp the lower flanges of the downstream stringer. The gritty surface of the I-beam bit into his fingers when he pushed off the fence, swinging his legs backwards. There wasn't much of a handhold. He'd have to swing his legs up again and hook his heels on the flanges to take the strain off his hands and arms. He began to rock back and forth, legs building into wider and wider swings until he was able to kick up with his heels. Now he could start to inch his way through the concertina.

Smock hung on the fence below him pulling on the concertina, trying to flatten it. "How you doing, Jarhead?" he said.

"Getting there. About halfway through. This wire doesn't snag as bad as the old stuff. But it's slicing the shit out of my legs. They're wet, and I'm not sweating that much yet."

"Roger, wet. You're dripping blood all over my arms."

"It's got to get better. My web gear and all this stuff slung on my back should help once I get farther into the wire."

"Just don't bleed to death before you make it through, Rip. And watch your head."

His head. There was no web gear to protect it. He tried to pull it up toward the stringer, out of the wire. That strained his neck and made everything twice as hard. He was sweating heavily. The sweat rolled into his cuts and they began to burn. He tried to ignore the pain and keep going, legs pushing past hundreds and hundreds of small razors, each sending new pain up through his body to replace the old pain as he pushed deeper and deeper into the wire.

Then he was through. Out of the wire. He shinnied a few more feet, tightened his grip on the I-beam, and let his legs drop free, clear of the wire. He was dangling at arm's length looking up at the underside of the bridge. The nearest pier was still ninety feet away. But the channels were clear. No more wire, thank God. He couldn't have fought that all the way out.

The firing built up again, upstream. There were new sounds along the north bank, dull clunks and pneumatic pops, as mortar rounds were dropped in and launched from their tubes. They had to be 82-millimeter mortars. Going for Binh's close-in positions along the south bank, saving the artillery for deeper targets . . .

A sharp, deafening crack came from the north bank, echoed almost immediately by a huge crash on the south. Tank fire. They had to have good targets; otherwise they wouldn't waste their ammo. Then the same pattern of noise started from the south bank. Tank fire was going both ways. It couldn't be Smock's doing, he thought. He's here at the bridge. Maybe Ley had finally decided to fight—on his own. If so, he'd be outgunned ten or twenty to one, even with every last tank of his on the line.

Ripley had to hurry. There was still a long way to go. Why weren't they shooting at him? They had to have seen him by now. His legs, anyway. Maybe the Soi Bien's covering fire was working. The NVA were keeping their heads down. Or maybe they just wanted a few grins before they knocked him off the bridge.

He began to hand-walk down the stringer. He got his legs working again, swaying, kicking, building momentum, just as he had swung down the monkey bars at Fort Benning. But he could get his whole hand around a monkey bar, not these I-beam flanges— and now he had to go five times as far. Reach. Grab. Reach. Grab. Pick it up. Reach. Grab. Reach. The satchel charges were swinging, pulling him out of his rhythm. Fifteen pounds apiece. He wished that he'd left them behind, but no, they were crucial. Like the grenades for detonators. The K-bar to cut fuze. And no Marine would go anywhere without his weapon and his water.

He tried not to worry or think too far ahead and concentrated on moving his body along the stringer, hoping his hands wouldn't give out or cramp up. At least nobody was shooting at him. They were about to lose their chance. Goodbye, assholes, he thought. He had almost reached the first pier.

He tightened his grip on the flanges and gathered strength to swing his legs up to the stringer again. With a pelvic thrust he kicked, a gymnast starting on the parallel bars. Nothing. He tried again, but could only twist slowly and painfully like a half-dead worm on a hook. His energy had left him without warning. Maybe he'd lost too much blood. His legs felt heavy and wooden and his arms were burning. His hands began to ache, the first sign of cramping. He knew if he stayed here at a dead hang they'd go numb and he would lose his grip, no matter how hard he tried to squeeze the girder.

The river sounded cool, rushing beneath him. If he were in that water it would wash over his skin and take away the heat and the sweat and the blood. He could slip off his gear and float light as driftwood with the water carrying him downstream and out of here.

But the water was three stories down, he knew that. With all his gear he would land like a boulder, crashing through the river's surface and sinking to the bottom. He'd never come up, the bridge would stand, Smock and the Soi Bien would fight like mad dogs for nothing. And he was up here dreaming about water.

He started swinging to build momentum for another kick. The swings got wider and wider and when he kicked again his feet touched metal for a second, then slipped. He tried again, driving his legs up with an effort beyond his limits so that for an instant he seemed to be outside his body watching it move. His boots flipped up and over the inboard flanges of the first channel. He wedged his heels against the vertical straps and pushed out. Now the strain had been taken off his arms and hands and he could rest a moment.

Then, working deliberately, he reached for the inboard girder and began to muscle his upper body into the channel between the first two stringers. He twisted around until his entire body was in the channel facing down, with his head pointed back toward the south bank of the river. He was practically spread-eagled, stretching to reach the lower flanges and shift his weight to his knees and elbows. In this position it was hard to unsling the satchel charges. Everything's taking so long, he thought. But finally he had them off and wedged into the channel. He began to inch his way slowly, painfully, back to the south bank. His legs were already ripped up. Now his knees and elbows would get it.

At the fence, Smock was waiting. He had managed to haul the first two boxes of TNT and satchel charges up the fence and push them through the razor wire into the channel. His arms and hands were bleeding profusely.

"I'd never make it without you, Major," Ripley said. "No way could I get through that wire every time."

"Yeah, we need each other bad. But let's keep

this show moving, pal. We can trade love notes later."

I guess he doesn't need any hand-holding, thought Ripley. Still spread-eagled across the channel, he grasped the bottom box and began to pull the load back toward the first pier. What a strain it was—two satchels on two full boxes of TNT, more than a hundred and eighty pounds, and the rough wood surface being dragged over metal textured like stucco. The boxes snagged every few inches, and he couldn't wrench them free because they might fall between the flanges they rested on. He didn't have time to go back for more. He had to pull the boxes straight over whatever was causing them to snag. Both his hands gripped and steadied the load, chancing no loss of control. Sweat began to run down his forehead and into his eyes, stinging them and blurring his vision. Should have rigged a sweatband first thing, he thought, and kept on pulling.

When he had hauled the boxes alongside the two satchel charges he brought earlier, he rested for a moment, muscles trembling. The boxes blocked his view of Smock and the south bank. He was alone. The thought of the major waiting for him seemed unreal. He checked his watch. Nearly noon. The round trip had taken over half an hour, and there were four more channels. Two more hours to go. How could he hold out, even if the NVA waited that long to come across the bridge?

He nestled the boxes of TNT into the earmuff satchel charge he had set up for the downstream stringer, then set up the charge for the second stringer, upstream. Now the first channel was completely blocked with explosives. It was time to move on.

He thought his next step through. He had to get a good grip on the second stringer, then drop below the steel for a moment while he swung to the third one. He couldn't hang on to both stringers at once—they were too far apart—so he would have to throw himself across the gap like an acrobat, grabbing in midair for the steel and praying the enemy was still asleep. That's enough to worry about for now, he thought.

But the enemy wasn't sleeping. As soon as Ripley dropped below the steel and exposed his lower body, firing from the north bank started again. Most of the shots clanged into the upstream stringer, but some riflemen had firing positions low on the riverbank. They were shooting up into the steel girders and their fire was ricocheting all over.

He tightened his hands around the flanges and began to talk himself through each step of the way into the next channel: Swing. Build momentum. Leap and grab. Get back into the steel, quickly. Catch the heels. Muscle into the channel. Push. Keep pushing. Do it.

He was safe again. In the steel. The minute he swung his legs up the firing stopped. As he crawled back to the south bank only an occasional harassing shot spanged against the girders. He felt rejuvenated. His senses were filed to a sharp edge. The enemy's challenge had brought new confidence and he thought he could go on forever.

It was like the commando course at Dartmoor. The Royal Marines did everything but shoot at him. In mid-winter, they loaded him down with a seventy-pound pack and ran him through bogs, icy streams, and underwater tunnels. Soaked to the bone and covered with mud, he had to do a six-mile run with full field gear against the clock. Once he reached his destination, the small-arms range, he had to fire and hit with every round in his magazine. One miss and the mission would be considered a failure. His chest was heaving while the clock ran on, but he held his aim. Do what you came to do. Performance counts. Nothing else matters. Do it.

Approaching the south bank again he could hear a steady stream of chatter coming from Smock. "One down, four to go, you crazy Jarhead. How you holding up? You look like hell."

"I'm okay," Ripley said. "Just have to catch my wind before I haul this ton of bricks back out there."

"Don't take all day. They might suddenly get brave and come across the river."

"Roger, speed," Ripley said. "Now, what about the detonators?"

"I'm looking. They've got to be around here somewhere."

"Jesus, man—those detonators are my life. You've got to find them!"

"Okay, okay. They're my life, too." Smock lost all his exuberance.

Because of the way Ripley had the demolitions angled across the stringers, the trips would be getting shorter, closer to the south bank in each channel. He thought he might even gain some time, but changed his mind when he began to drag the next boxes of TNT. They seemed twice as heavy as the first. He was grunting out loud with each pull.

The second trip wound up taking as long as the first. His leap to the third channel set off another burst of fire, but the ricochets came no closer. He couldn't believe that North Vietnamese regulars were such lousy shots. That they wouldn't have worked themselves into better firing positions under the bridge. Maybe the Soi Bien had them pinned in their fighting holes, afraid to expose themselves long enough to take well-aimed shots. Keep them ducking, he thought.

By the time he muscled his way back into the steel and worked his body around into a spread eagle he was gasping for breath like a steam engine. Over his own breathing he could just hear Smock with his infield chatter about everything and nothing.

"Where are you, Rip? Is that you huffing and puffing out there? Or is that snoring? What are you doing, taking a nap with your bridge on? Get moving, Pokey, the phone's ringing . . ."

Good old Smock, the cheerleader. They were working on this together. He hoped the NVA didn't get him, find him wounded by the bridge and capture him. Or me either, he thought.

"Halfway there, Marine. Press on!"

Despite the energizing effect of Smock's talk and the enemy's fire, his pace continued to slow over the next hour and a half. After pulling the final boxes of TNT into place and rigging the final earmuff charge in the upstream channel, he had only a short hand-walk back to the south bank, pursued by relentless but ineffective fire. He swung his legs up, hooked his heels over the lower flanges of the upstream stringer, and worked his body through the concertina wire. It was easier this time because Smock had tamped it down. Then he dropped to the ground near the abutment and lay there doubled over, fighting for breath.

Smock pounded him on the back. "I can't believe you, you crazy sonofabitch! Wiring a bridge by the numbers."

"That's the problem. It ain't wired yet. We still have to set it off. Find any detonators?"

"How about these?" Smock held up a container of percussion blasting caps. "And this?" He pointed to a coil of primer cord.

"Shit hot, Major! Where'd you find them?"

"Near the bottom of the demo boxes," Smock said. "Just had to pull enough of them away."

"Electrical caps are more reliable, but these'll do fine. A lot better than a goddamn jury-rigged grenade detonator with a four-second getaway time and a guaranteed swim in the river. Did you find any crimpers?"

"What?"

"They look like pliers. They're to crimp the blasting cap onto the primer cord."

"Didn't see anything like that lying around . . ."

So they would have to do it the hard way. The crazy way. Every time they were just about there, they came up short. "Okay, then," Ripley said, "you're about to see a classic demo of how not to set a time fuze. Better stand back a ways if you don't want the inside of my head spattered all over you."

"Knock it off, Rip. What do you mean?"

"I mean I need those miserable crimpers to measure the primer cord and calculate the approximate burn time. Most of all I need them because no demo man who values his own personal ass would ever try to attach a detonator to primer cord without them."

During hands-on demo training in Malaya, the color sergeant had been most emphatic, speaking with the authority of his Special Boat Service, the elite frogmen of the Royal Marines. "Right, lads. Now pay attention. You can't serve the Queen if blown to bits. This shiny cylinder is a detonator, sometimes called a blasting cap. Never clutch this little bugger too firmly in your hand, or place it next to anything you don't wish to have removed.

"Hold the detonator gently, between thumb and forefinger. Then grip it lightly, in precisely the right spot, with your crimpers. If you grip the detonator too far away from the open end, you might set the treacherous thing off. Too far toward the open end and you might fix the cap too loosely to the primer cord; that could cause it to fall off or fail to detonate.

"Once you have the crimpers in the right place,

move them, the detonator, and the primer cord down and away—behind your best natural blast absorber, the gluteus maximus. Then, turning your head away, gradually tighten your grip until the detonator is crimped securely to the primer cord. That way if you've miscalculated, you'll only lose a few fingers and a chunk of your arse. Vital organs will remain intact."

The old color sergeant would go crazy if he could see this, Ripley thought.

"So what do you do when you don't have crimpers?" Smock was saying, hesitantly, as if sensing that he wouldn't like the answer.

"The old miners used to call it jawboning."

"Ho-ly—"

"But before we get to that," Ripley said, "I've got to measure and cut this primer cord. It's supposed to burn about a foot a minute. To do it right, we should burn a sample length and time it. But we don't have crimpers to measure precise six-inch increments, and we don't have enough time to screw around with that anyway."

"What do we do, then?"

"Field expedient. One arm's length measured from the center of my chest is roughly three feet. I'm going to set a thirty-minute fuze in each of the outboard channels. I don't like to give the enemy that much time, but he's been sitting around all day with his thumb up his bum and his mind in neutral, so maybe a few more minutes won't matter. And I may need every second of that delay to finish up both fuzes and get off the bridge before it blows. So ten arm's lengths should give me thirty minutes, more or less."

He quickly measured and cut the primer cord, then carefully pulled the first detonator from its box. He inserted the end of the primer cord into the open end of the shiny cap and stared at it intently for a moment. At Ranger school, the instructor had placed a detonator inside a softball and lit it off. The explosion flung cover, stuffing, and string all over the place. He imagined his hair, teeth, and eyeballs spewed out like that.

"Stand back, Major. Here we go." He placed the detonator inside his mouth with the open end facing out. The primer cord ran from his mouth down to a coil on the ground. With his teeth, he searched the surface of the detonator gingerly for just the right spot to crimp it. The cylinder was huge in his mouth and he felt like gagging. When his teeth found the rim he slid the detonator a minute distance out. Then he bit, bearing down slowly, tightening his grip. The detonator tasted awful, like aluminum. His teeth began to ache.

When he had crimped the detonator, he eased it out of his mouth. Smock was leaning away, with his face averted. His shoulders were hunched and his palms raised, a boxer against the ropes.

"Want to give it a try, Major?" Ripley said.

"One lunatic on this working party is enough."

"I agree. Watch me do it again."

He knew the second time would be easier but he

wasn't going to get sloppy, not with the memory of that softball. After he crimped the next one he slung a coil of primer cord over each shoulder and ran the ends, capped with detonators, into his breast pockets. Then he buttoned the pockets carefully.

"What a half-assed way to carry detonators," he said. "And what a half-assed way to rig them. This would get me thrown out of anybody's demo school." Smock didn't answer. He seemed to be in shock.

It's time, Ripley thought. He had to go back out there. He had to go back out and he knew the enemy was waiting for him. "So long, Major," he said, silently praying to God to help him get there, and back, in one piece.

*H*e worked his way back through the wire, unseen by infantry-men on either bank of the river. Firing had dwindled to sporadic rifle shots. The NVA's automatic weapons were silent, lying in wait for him. He wished Binh's people were able to see him. Then he could give them a heads-up before dropping beneath the steel and they could start up a base of fire. Buy him a few seconds. It had worked before, when he was coming down the hill. But he was much closer to the Northerners now. They probably had the upstream stringer centered in their sights.

He could try to shinny down the girder, but that would take forever and sooner or later they would spot him. Then when he had to drop down and swing into the channel they would have him bore-sighted. He decided to do it the old way, moving hand over hand and depending on the Soi Bien to be quick on the uptake.

When he emerged from the wire he breathed deeply, then dropped beneath the girder. The ene-my's response was immediate and far heavier than before. The sound of hundreds of ricochets rang through the stringers, drowning individual hits the way a downpour overwhelms a raindrop. This time, answering volleys from the south bank didn't slow the Northerners down.

After pulling on the concertina Smock remained clinging to the sapper fence, exposed to fire while he yelled encouragement. It helped Ripley keep up his speed, and speed was his only hope. He chanted rhythmically to build momentum. "Je-sus Ma-ry get me there. Jesus-Mary-get-me-there. JesusMaryget-methere . . ."

He reached the upstream box of TNT and kicked up, heels hooking the I-beam flanges on the first try. He was working his upper body into the channel when, less than two feet from where his left hand grasped the lower flange, a tank round hit.

The tank's angle of fire was too sharp for the round to detonate on contact with the bridge. It glanced off the stringer's vertical strap and plowed into the south bank, exploding with a violent crash. The noise and concussion spread out in a great wave, echoing off the riverbanks and under the bridge and traveling through the girders so they vibrated like a giant bell.

He almost lost his grip on the flanges and had to press his heels into the steel as hard as he could to regain control. Holy Mother of God, they've got me this time, he thought.

It must have been the T-54 that sergeant damaged earlier in the day with a LAAW. The turret was probably still jammed, but the commander could point his immobilized main gun by twisting the tank on its tracks. It would be easy to zero in on the upstream stringer from a position low on the riverbank.

Ley's tanks remained silent. Binh's infantry had already used up the LAAWs and Ripley could hear their small-arms fire pinging off the T-54's armor, fleas off the hide of an elephant. Meanwhile the small-arms fire from the north bank had built to a crescendo, as though the NVA sensed that this was their final chance to stop Ripley. Binh's men were unable to stifle the heavy fire with their own.

Inside the channel, rounds clanging around him, Ripley tried to concentrate. Working methodically, he pulled back the canvas top of the satchel charge that was wedged between the upstream girder and the top of the first demo box. With his K-bar he dug a hole in the creamy C-4 explosive and buried the detonator attached to one of his coils of primer cord.

Gingerly, he packed C-4 around the detonator to hold it in place. Using his K-bar again, he cut into the other end of the primer, about two inches deep. Next he fumbled in his large cargo pocket for a plastic bag like the one he kept his family snapshots in.

The snapshots. If only he could have another look at them now. But he knew that would just take time and increase his chances of failing. Of dying. He had to press on or he would never see them again. Dead, he would be nothing more than a memory, a few beat-up personal effects sent home. Not even those, if his body was recovered by the North Vietnamese. He thought about a scrounging NVA soldier cutting off his finger to get his wedding ring. Then he caught himself daydreaming and drove his attention back to the task at hand. He pulled out the plastic bag. It contained several books of C-ration matches with olive covers and bold black lettering that began, "THESE MATCHES HAVE BEEN DESIGNED TO LIGHT IN DAMP CLIMATES . . ." They better work, he thought. He didn't have a fuze lighter to do the job right. At least he was out of the wind.

He tore off a match and inserted it headfirst in the split end of the primer. Striking a second match, he lit the torn end of the first one and watched it burn down toward the phosphorus-coated tip. The tip flared, and the cord began to burn like a small Fourth of July sparkler. He let the roll of cord fall through the gap between the stringers. Uncoiling, it danced above the water, the lit end a darting firefly.

Now it was three quick leaps to the downstream

channel. The firing grew heavy again as he dropped below the steel. Over the din he could still hear Smock. "Crazy Jarhead, move your ass!"

They weren't going to get him now. He was winning. He reached the downstream stringer and swung back into the steel, muscling himself up with a surge of energy. Anything's better than hauling those ten-ton boxes down channels, he thought. But he still had to beat the burning fuze. He still had to be careful. He couldn't get sloppy and drop his K-bar. Not when he was so close to the end.

He went to work on the second fuze, packing the detonator carefully into the satchel charge. Working as rapidly as possible without sacrificing control, he split the bitter end of the primer cord and inserted another paper match headfirst. After he lit it, the match stem glowed briefly, then died. Was he sweating on the matches, making them too wet? He found a dry patch on his trousers and wiped his hands before pulling another match from the book and inserting it in the split primer. "Burn, damnit, burn," he whispered, bending close to his work. The match flared, the flame worked up the stem. Then the primer cord ignited in bright sparkles.

He didn't waste any time dropping the coil of primer and lowering himself beneath the steel for the final trip back to the south bank. This time, however, the firing didn't intensify. Either they'd lost him or they were getting ready to storm across the bridge.

He fought off that thought, repeating his cadenced chant. "Je-sus Ma-ry get me there. Jesus-

Mary-get-me-there. JesusMarygetmethere." Over the sound of his voice he heard Smock yelling something, and then realized it was a prayer. Smock was praying out loud.

He was almost there. He reached the concertina, propelled himself up and into it, and fought through one last time while Smock pulled it down to make an opening. Clear of the sapper fence, he let his legs dangle briefly beneath the steel before dropping to the ground and collapsing in a tattered, bloody heap near the bridge abutment.

"You did it, you crazy sonofabitch! Right by the book. Right by the numbers," Smock said.

"Can't talk. Just let me lie here."

"We've got to clear out before the bridge blows."

"There's still time," Ripley said. "Ten or twenty minutes. Have to rest . . ."

"Don't fade on me, Rip. Not after all this. You're too damn heavy to carry."

"I'm okay, just need to catch my breath." But he wasn't. His arms felt as if they'd been pulled from their sockets. He couldn't have lifted a bottle of beer if given the chance. He was so tired, melting into the ground . . .

Smock tapped him on the back. "Look what I found. But you don't need them now." He pointed to a box of electrical detonators.

Painfully, Ripley raised himself on an elbow. "Where were they when I needed them?" he said. He glanced in the direction of the time fuzes but he was too far away to see if they were still burning.

They had to be. They never went out once they were lit. How much time was left? Twenty minutes? Fifteen? He'd lost track.

It would be stupid to take those caps back out if the bridge was going to blow anyway. But what if it didn't? To be sure, they needed a backup. He had to rig the electrical charge so there wouldn't be any doubt.

I've been poking fate in the ass all day, he thought, why quit now? The job wouldn't be over until they had tried everything. Commandos didn't botch a job and go home. If they botched this, nobody would make it home.

He was going out again.

NINE

*H*e opened the box of detonators and removed five electrical caps, each with a long lead wire attached.

"What are you doing now, for Chrissakes?" Smock said. "Let's get the hell out of here."

"I have to go back out on the bridge. Got to set the backup."

Smock raised his hands, palms facing the sky. "What, going by the book again? Screw the book! There's no time to go back. Those goddamn fuzes have got to be burning. One of them, anyway. I can see it."

"Don't want to take the chance," Ripley said. "There's time if I hurry. Help me back through the wire, okay?"

"You scare me, Rip."

"I know. You told me."

Smock couldn't be half as scared as he was. That cold knot of fear had lodged in his stomach and the arches of his feet ached, as though he'd been walking along the peak of a rooftop. He should have had the job finished by now and be running back uphill to the bunker, but there was no real choice.

"Major," he said, "you better not stick around here, in case she blows. How about hauling some demo over to the old French bridge? Just stay low. You should be in defilade most of the way. The Marines will cover you. Then when this monster goes the French bridge will go with it. Sympathetic detonation."

"Are you sure you know what you're doing?" Smock said, squinting at Ripley out of the corners of his eyes.

"I know exactly what I'm doing. Help me round up some comm wire and get ready to go back out there."

The area was crisscrossed with communications wire that had once linked field telephones. Ripley began to pull on a long strand leading back to the Dye Marker bunker, looping it into a coil he could carry over his shoulder. When he had several hundred feet, he severed the light wire with his K-bar and skinned back the black insulation to uncover two interior wires, one copper and one silver. Then he wrapped each detonator in its lead wire and placed it in his shirt pocket. Three went in the left pocket, two in the right.

This was not the way to do it. Electrical caps were just as touchy as percussion caps. Touchier, in some ways. Swimming ashore in frogman training, he'd carried one in his mouth—two at most—to ensure a smooth ride. Carrying two and even three in his pockets where they could bang into each other was dumb. But there was no time for more than one trip, maybe not even one.

The ARVN engineers had left behind a repair kit with black plastic tape. Not as good as electrician's tape, but it wouldn't have to protect the splice forever.

"I'm ready, Major," Ripley said. "How about a hand?"

"Okay. Let's get rolling so we can haul ass out of here."

"Just pull the wire down and help get me started. Then you can start working on the French bridge."

He cleared the razor wire, then hung below the steel and with his hands moving along the upstream stringer approached the nearest box of demolitions. He was tense, braced for the first burst of gunfire, but none came. Maybe they thought he'd finished. Nobody in his right mind would set the fuzes twice. Or maybe they'd finally moved from their holes and were getting ready to charge the bridge.

Then a single bullet hit the girder, much too close, spanging off the steel a split second before he heard the crack of a rifle shot from the north bank. They'd dug up a sniper to come after him. Another bee swarm of ricochets swept in and around him. I've finally gone and done it this time, he thought. Got myself right in the middle of a spark factory with my pockets full of electrical caps.

But he was almost there. He kicked up, hooked his heels, reached over and worked his body into the steel, lead-limbed. Black dots swam before his eyes. He slumped forward in the channel. Then his head grazed the vertical strap of an I-beam and he jerked back as though he'd touched an electrified fence. He had passed out. Adrenaline started pumping through his veins and his body went racing ahead of his mind, still groggy from sleep. He wondered how long he'd been out, if he'd dropped completely off. He looked at the fuze, but couldn't calculate how much was still unburned.

He had to hurry. His hands were cramping up again. His fingers felt stiff, useless as a bunch of twigs. Fumbling with his K-bar, he dug a hole in the C-4 for the first electrical cap. Then he stopped and tried to relax the muscles in his hand, shaking it like a wrestler warming up. He couldn't afford to lose control of the blade—couldn't afford to create any sparks. He buried the detonator and molded C-4 around it as he had done with the percussion caps, leaving the lead wire with its metal shunt to protrude from the satchel charge. He tucked the end of the lead wire into his pistol belt and lowered himself below the steel for the leap to the next channel. The firing intensified, but he no longer feared getting hit. Now he had to worry about sparks. If the rounds landed any closer they would set off the detonators in a second. All it would take was one lucky shot. But it would do the enemy in, too. There was some comfort in that.

He still couldn't figure out why they weren't rushing the bridge. Why they were just sitting back and taking potshots at him. Maybe Smock had spooked them when he destroyed six of their tanks. Maybe they thought they were facing a couple of brigades on the south bank instead of a couple hundred men, and were waiting for more infantry to move up for the assault. Christ, the NVA must have two hundred tanks, he thought. All they had to do was get one or two across the river and it was over.

He had to get back to business. How to hook up the electrical charges? If he wired the five caps in series, they would be like a string of Christmas lights—one break in the wire and they'd all go. He had to set up the circuit in parallel. Splice all five leads into a single yoke. Then splice that into the comm wire and run the comm wire back to shore.

He began to work with methodical haste. He pulled back the canvas top of a satchel charge and buried an electrical cap in the C-4. Paying out lead wire from the detonator, he removed the metal shunt and skinned back insulation to expose the two interior wires. These he spliced to the interior wires of the comm line—hot wires first, copper to copper, then ground wires, silver to silver. After wrapping the splice with plastic tape, he swung into the next channel to repeat the process.

His brief nap had given him a headache. Distracted, he wondered whether he should give it up now that two electrical caps were in place. The downstream fuze still sparkled, more than half gone. He couldn't see the upstream fuze, the one he'd lit first. Then he forced his attention back to the task at hand. There was no time to waste. He still had three caps to go and he wouldn't win his race by staying in the channel thinking about it. He dropped below the channel, swung across, and pulled himself into the steel of the neighboring channel, trying to forget the fuzes and the fear that they might finish burning early.

Still, his mind wandered. He thought of his wife and the telegram they'd send, like the one when his brother's plane crashed: "THE SECRETARY OF THE NAVY REGRETS TO INFORM YOU . . . KILLED IN ACTION IN THE DEFENSE OF FREEDOM . . . BODY NOT RECOVERED . . . HIS MANY FRIENDS JOIN ME AND THE PRESIDENT IN EXPRESSING OUR SORROW AT YOUR PROFOUND LOSS . . ." At the end of the memorial service they'd give her a flag neatly folded in a triangle. All the red would be tucked out of sight, white stars only staring from the deep blue field.

"YOU MAY BE COMFORTED IN YOUR LOSS BY REALIZING THAT HE WAS LAST SEEN PERFORMING HIS DUTY AT GREAT PERSONAL RISK, AND THAT HIS ACCOMPLISH-

MENTS . . ." What accomplishments? The bloody bridge might not blow. "YOU HAVE THE THANKS OF A GRATEFUL NATION." She wouldn't need that.

He had to get back to his family, and he had to do it by finishing this up. By concentrating on the job and letting go of the fear. "Let go," he said out loud. Breathe deep. Make it disappear. Do it.

He moved on, caught up now in the mechanics of his task. He planted detonators in three more satchel charges and ran their lead wires into the makeshift yoke, splicing carefully, then taping. The yoke bulged with layer upon layer of black plastic tape. It looked like a huge spider upside down, legs clutching the underside of the bridge in a fatal embrace.

As he returned to shore hand over hand, trailing one of the spider's long legs, another burst of fire erupted from the north bank. He tensed, then relaxed. There were no ricochets. Ricochets would have come before the sound of gunfire. They were firing at someone else.

Smock. Maybe they had spotted him moving demo to the French bridge. Only a couple of boxes were needed there and he worried that Smock might be exposing himself unnecessarily by hauling more.

Then he heard the major yelling across the river like a crazy man. "Can't kill a tanker, bastards!" And at that moment he sensed that Smock would survive, as though the power of his voice, carrying over the sound of gunfire, were also a shield protecting him from incoming rounds.

They started firing at Ripley as well. This time some of the fire came from downstream where enemy riflemen had a better shot at him. But they were too late, nothing could stop him now, he was invulnerable like Smock. "Fire away, you miserable sons of bitches!" he screamed in one final burst of energy. "Last chance!"

Now Smock was praying under the bridge in a loud unrestrained voice, wild man thundering at the heavens. Ripley squirmed through the wire and collapsed on the ground, too tired to raise his head.

The major pounced on him, shaking his shoulders violently. "Get up, Rip! We can't stay here! The fuze has already burned too long. Binh's people are ready to cover us while we go back up the hill."

Painfully, he pulled himself into a kneeling position. He shouldered the coil of communications wire and hauled himself up on unsteady legs. Then he gave a slashing arm signal and the Soi Bien unleashed their heaviest base of fire yet. He and Smock broke from cover, heading uphill with dreamlike slowness. The Marines yelled encouragement, voices mounting in volume and pitch until they were a rhythmic screeching that pierced the din of battle. *"Dai-uy Dien! Dai-uy Dien! Dai-uy Dien!"* Captain Crazy.

He had to pay out the comm wire as he moved, which slowed him down even more than the pain. His body was a large resisting mass that he had to drag along like the boxes of TNT. His legs could barely support him as he staggered across the uneven

ground. Small geysers of dirt from incoming rounds shot up around him as if the ground underneath were boiling up. For an instant he thought the bullets landing in front of him had passed clean through his body, that he was in fact invulnerable. Was he numb? Was that it, bullets going through him without his feeling them? Or was he dead, in purgatory, running on an endless treadmill?

TEN

*T*hey dove to the ground behind the Dye Marker bunker as the Vietnamese chant continued, rising and falling like the two-tone siren of an emergency vehicle: "*Dai-uy. Dai-uy. Dai-uy.* Die we. Die we. Die. We die . . ." Then word sped down the firing line that the *co-van* and the other American were safe and the chant exploded into a sustained cheer.

The two of them lay there, side by side, gasping. "They think it's over," Ripley said to Smock when he had his breath back. "They think we've won. But the bridge is still standing."

"It'll blow," Smock said. He was checking himself for bullet holes.

Ripley did the same, finding nothing but the blood and sweat already caked on his skin. So he was back among the living.

Nha ran up with a grin so big it exposed his upper gumline. He huddled close to the bunker's sandbags, radio handset pressed to his ear.

For Ripley, having Nha back was like finding something old and familiar and comfortable. "Glad to see me, little brother?" he said, grabbing him by the shoulder.

"Nha think *Dai-uy bi chet. Fini. Het roi.* Say on radio."

"Reported me dead? Tell them *co-van* never die. Never happen." Nha nodded vigorously and began talking into the handset.

Smock was lying on his back now, sweating heavily. Rivulets rolled down his cheeks and left muddy streaks across them. "I feel like I've had three years of war packed into the last three hours."

"All in a day's work for a grunt."

"Rip, this is a no-shitter. I haven't seen anything like this in two full combat tours as a tanker. Can I die here peacefully, or are you going to run my ass some more?"

"What did I tell you, Major? Stick with me and someday you'll wear shoes. Might even learn a few things."

"Yeah, well, learning from a grunt is one thing," Smock said, "but I sure as hell don't want to die like one. Just get me safely back inside a tank and I'll mention you in my will."

"Look, we did this together. Almost, that is. There's still more."

"Now what?" Smock covered his ears. Hear no evil . . .

"I don't trust those time fuzes. It's been too long. We have to light off this sonofabitch with the electrical caps. We need a power source. Did you see a small metal box lying around back there? With a twist handle?"

Smock rolled over and raised himself on two elbows. "What the hell are you talking about? I found two boxes of detonators and thought I was doing pretty good. Now you want me to find you a box with a handle?"

"I didn't think there'd be one. Those suckers are hard to come by. But we've got to find another power source or that last trip out on the bridge was a big waste of time."

He moved out to begin the search, Nha trailing him. As soon as he turned the back corner of the bunker, he saw a burning vehicle near the crest of the hill. A jeep had been knocked on its side by an exploding artillery round. Flames curled around the engine and forward part of the chassis, away from the gas tank. Black smoke rose steadily from the two upper tires.

It wasn't much of a hellbox. The battery would

be under the driver's seat and hard to get to, especially with the metal so hot. But it would have to do. At least it was in defilade. He could crawl right up to it without the enemy seeing him.

He dropped on all fours and worked his way up to the jeep, paying out communications wire behind him. When he got close enough he saw that the explosion had knocked the front seat forward. The battery was exposed, still seated firmly in its housing. He could reach it.

The key sat in the ignition. There was no driver. With his K-bar he severed the paid-out comm wire from the rest of the coil and skinned back several inches of insulation, exposing the two wires inside. Then he wrapped the copper wire around the battery's positive terminal. The heat coming from the jeep was intense. Could it make the battery blow up in his face?

He touched the silver wire to the negative terminal with great care, expecting a spark, but nothing happened. Maybe the terminals were crusted. He unhooked the copper wire. With his K-bar he scraped away rust and a powdery-white sodium buildup, digging into the soft metal of the terminals. Then he tried again, wrapping the copper wire around the positive terminal and touching the silver to the negative.

Still nothing. What was wrong? There should have been enough juice in the battery to pop an electrical cap twenty miles away. Did he have the terminals backwards? He switched wires, just to be sure, wrapping the copper around the negative terminal and touching the silver to the positive. Again, no result. His Naval Academy diploma said he was supposed to be an electrical engineer and he couldn't even light off a blasting cap.

He decided to check the battery for juice. He bridged the terminals, producing a spark that jumped out and bit him. No, the battery wasn't drained. Maybe he had pulled the wire across something sharp and cut it. Maybe the wire had been cut by gunfire. Or were the caps simply no good after sitting out in the field for months?

He began to wonder why everything he touched was turning sour. Why nothing worked, even when he went right by the book. Hanging my ass out in the wind for nothing, he thought bitterly. A rotten goddamn lousy dream. They were all going to die anyway.

He would have to call Brigade and warn them. There might still be time left for the others to regroup farther south, though he and the Soi Bien had to stay here. Binh would never pull back. He'd already made that clear. Maybe they could buy the rest of the Third Division some time by fighting and dying along the river.

Maybe they could pile up a few NVA tanks on the bridge and delay their crossing. Smock could do that. If the major squeezes even a light section of tanks out of Ley, I'll buy him a truckload of beer, Ripley thought, knowing it wasn't likely.

He looked south down Highway 1, past the triangle where it intersected Highway 9. Two figures were in the middle of the road walking toward him. He wondered why they weren't using cover and decided it was because they knew he had failed. It was all over, why bother? The figures came closer and he saw they were Binh and Jack. When he could see their faces more clearly he realized he'd been wrong, they hadn't given up. They were looking at the river, trying to figure out how to defend the south bank, without thinking of him. He felt suddenly as though he were in a movie theater and that nothing he did would make the slightest difference to the actors on the screen or the story they were playing out. He had ceased to exist. They had put their faith in him and he had failed. He wished that if he died they would somehow discover he had gone out on the bridge that extra time.

He knew if he walked up to them right now and told them they were going to die, they wouldn't believe him. They didn't think that way. Jack never worried about anything that didn't stare him in the face, and not much then. Binh, the scarred sea wolf, would die at his post with no forethought of death, along with his seven hundred Marines or however many were left. He would never show his back to an adversary. He would absorb the enemy's fire and fury, ennobled by his sacrifice. It would become his memorial. He and his Marines would press on, with or without Ripley, fighting a war that had lasted a thousand years and would continue for many more.

148

As they approached, Binh was still staring at the river, but Three-Finger Jack looked straight at the *co-van* and smiled his strange half-smile. The worse things got, the happier he seemed to be. But to Ripley, the look meant much more than that. The space surrounding him was like a huge roll of insulation keeping him apart from the others and Jack's smile cut through it, as cleanly and easily as his knife cut through his finger that time he had proved himself.

Down Highway 9 to the west Ripley could see little but destruction from the morning's artillery bombardment: great chunks of mortar and cinder block, sheets of corrugated tin riddled with holes and twisted into bizarre shapes, and protruding through the rubble at odd angles, the legs and arms of smashed furniture. Fires burned everywhere. Low-lying smoke blocked the sun. There was no connection between this scarred landscape and any place on earth. A sullen silence hung over Dong Ha, broken only by desultory small-arms fire and the occasional dull thump of an exploding artillery or mortar round.

From across the river he heard the sound of tanks starting up, getting ready to make their move. When the firing resumed, they would be kicking off an assault across the bridge.

The futility of it all swept over him with renewed force. What were they coming across the bridge to capture? A city? No, a city dump. A graveyard. A churned-up field filled with thousands upon thousands of bodies. City of the dead, awaiting liberation by its neighbors from the North.

From the smoky pall over Highway 9 a solitary figure emerged, a shade escaped from Hades searching for its former home. The apparition was limping. Little by little, he was able to make out the features of a woman. She had a slender, almost frail figure and the unstooped posture of a young woman. But her skin was leathery and lined and her eyes stared ahead, at nothing, having already seen more than most humans could stand. Her body continued to function for one reason only and that was to keep moving on. She was leaning on a large pole, favoring her right foot.

A soft gray cloth framed her face, and she wore a loose robe of the same material, heavily soiled and damp from recent rains. She carried a small pack on her back. A sling held an infant to her breast.

When she reached the triangle the woman turned right, limping down Highway 1 to the south. It was then that he saw she was missing her right foot, maybe part of her leg—he couldn't tell because of the robe. She had strapped some sort of stake to her thigh, a makeshift limb to help her move. No matter how far she walks she'll never get away, he thought.

Another, smaller figure took shape through the haze, a young girl dressed in rags. Her eyes were slits and her mouth was open in a permanent wail. She was trying to keep up with her mother, but her mother no longer knew she was there.

He wanted to call to the child and tell her where her mother had gone, but he couldn't remember the Vietnamese words. Then a mortar round hit the road behind her and he was up and running, realizing she would never make it on her own. At the last instant, she looked up and saw him. Her wailing stopped and her eyes widened in terror; she was screaming silently. He scooped her up from the front and her small legs flopped like a Raggedy Ann doll's. His momentum carried them a few steps, then he pivoted and broke into a full run for the crossroad. Seconds later, he rounded the corner onto Highway 1.

He had almost reached the little girl's mother when the bridge blew.

It was the shock wave that came first, not the noise. The two of them went flying as if a powerful hand had slapped them from behind. His body was moving through the air faster than his legs could have taken it, faster than he ever could have run.

Then the noise arrived, growing louder and louder in a series of explosions that soon merged in a steady roar and branded itself into him. He clung to the girl and grunted as his shoulder slammed against the stony roadside. They tumbled into a ditch, their fall cushioned by the bodies of the dead.

The girl had landed on top of him. For an instant she lay there, stunned. Then without a sound she scrambled to her bare feet and ran away.

Large, irregular chunks of debris hurtled through the air. Smaller pieces spun upward, rising hundreds of feet before falling back to earth in random patterns like handfuls of flung jacks. They thudded into the streets and clattered against the gnarled sheets of tin roofing.

The girl was wandering in the road now. He left the ditch and carried her to a nearby doorway that provided overhead cover. She was still too shaken to cry or scream. Then he raced back to the highway, heading for the crest of the hill to take his first good look at what remained of the bridge.

The time fuzes had done the job after all. The near span had dropped into the river, leaving a hundred-foot gap between the south bank and the rest of the bridge. The force of the explosion had gouged out a large section of the bank and a pressure wave was rising and expanding, upstream and downstream and across the river. The bridge's thick timbers were on fire, and a cloud of gray smoke mushroomed from them, intensifying the pall over Dong Ha.

The old French bridge was cut too. Whatever Smock dragged over there had packed enough explosive force.

The enemy would never get across now. Not here, anyway.

Smock came running uphill and stood beside him on the crest. "Thank God for your Ranger training," he said. "Never could have done it myself. I can't believe it. Neither will my boss."

"I had some other training too," Ripley said. "But we did it together. You were with me the whole way." They started hugging and pounding each other on the back and it was better than words. Nothing they could say would ever match how they felt.

Right out in the open, they celebrated. They were still under the enemy's guns but it didn't matter anymore. They had hung it all out to foil him and they'd won. They felt invulnerable again, just the way they had while racing back from the bridge.

Then Three-Finger Jack burst out of the haze, running toward them at full speed. They'd barely realized who he was before he cut them down with a rolling body block, screaming, "*Dai-uy* crazy! *Bi chet! Het roi!*" You'll die.

As they stumbled back to the bunker, where Nha and Binh were waiting, Jack hovered over them like a proud but anxious father. He needn't have bothered. The enemy's fire had come to a complete stop as soon as the bridge blew. On the north bank tanks stood bumper to bumper, engines stopped, hatches open. Tank commanders were gazing up at the billowing smoke, looking for signs of hostile aircraft.

Along the south bank Vietnamese Marines were climbing out of their fighting holes, waving their helmets over their heads and cheering. They acted as though the war were over.

Ripley wasn't convinced. As soon as a destroyer on the gun line could be raised he was going to call in more fire on the NVA tanks, while they were stacked up on the north bank. But first he had to call Brigade. "*Nha! Lai day!*"

Nha brought the radio. Ripley keyed the handset. "Leatherneck, this is Delta. The bridge is down. I say again, the bridge is down. She's in the river. They won't cross at Dong Ha. They'll have to come by way of Tijuana now. Over."

"Roger, Delta. We can see the smoke from here. What the hell did you do, nuke it? We're breathing a lot easier now. Well done . . . Well done . . ."

Then he remembered the little girl and postponed the naval gunfire request. He gave the handset to Nha and ran back to the triangle where Highways 9 and 1 intersected, but she was nowhere in sight. He tried to recall which doorway he had left her in, afraid of what he might find if he located her.

He stared down Highway 1. It was deserted. Nothing moved but small trails of smoke rising from shattered vehicles and overturned carts and the bodies of the dead.

Then he saw them in the distance, two figures receding into the translucent haze. The woman pulled her foot along painfully, a bird dragging a broken wing. The child trudged alongside.

ELEVEN

*T*he battle was in a state of suspension. The Soi Bien continued to leave their fighting holes, condemned men granted a reprieve from a certain sentence of death. They stood up and walked about, ignoring the enemy only a few hundred feet across the river. They were oblivious to danger. The new moat that confounded the Northerners might have been a thousand miles wide, and the absence of fire from the far bank seemed to say that for the time being the enemy acknowledged—even accepted—the situation.

They streamed up the hill toward Ripley, gaunt men in muddy boots, helmets in hand. Their soft sing-song voices were soothing to him. *"Cam on, Dai-uy."* Thanks, Captain. *"Bac-Viet het roi."* The North Vietnamese are through.

They can't talk that way to their own officers, he thought. The social gulf was too great.

He was propped against the bunker holding his hand out, passively, without strength to return the handshakes some gave him. Others patted his bloodied knees, which showed through torn trousers. Perhaps they were doing it for luck. Touch a survivor and survive.

Here he was in what was almost a receiving line and he didn't even have the strength to smile. He was drooping like an old street bum. He began to feel the pain in his forearms, scorched by the heat of the burning jeep, and the cuts from his last trip through the wire oozing new blood through the older, caked blood. He'd been running on adrenaline for God knows how long and he couldn't remember the last time he'd eaten. His eyes started to close.

"Dai-uy phai di bac-si!" he heard someone shout. It sounded like Jack, calling for the doctor. But the doctor was down by the river trying to save wounded Marines.

Ripley sagged against the bunker. He was slipping beneath the surface of a dark sea, unable to resist the urge to let go. Voices swam around him, distant, muffled. He opened his eyes halfway and saw

Nha and Jack kneeling beside him. Jack unstrapped his helmet for use as a makeshift pillow, then held his head up at the back of the neck while he and Nha lowered him into a reclining position.

The bodyguard left and returned with a can of the condensed milk they used for sweetening coffee. He punched a hole in the top of the can, twisting his fighting knife into it until it was large enough for his right trigger finger. Then he pulled Ripley's jaw down and used his finger to spoon the syrupy liquid into his mouth.

Before long, he started coming around. He lay on the ground dead tired but growing more alert. Finally he lifted his head, then sat up to see what was happening on the other side of the river. It was a scene of paralysis and confusion. The NVA column had piled up on itself, and the roadway leading to the bridge looked like a freeway after a multi-car collision. Now it would take the enemy days or weeks—instead of hours—to get to Hue. Meanwhile, stranded like that, he was an inviting target for U.S. naval guns offshore and for American and South Vietnamese aircraft whose northward flight would stretch over friendly territory until the moment came to strike. For the first time since his offensive began, he had little opportunity to strike back.

The NVA tankers must have sensed it. Some were beginning to pull their vehicles out of line, despite the hazards of off-road marshes and rice paddies. They backed and turned, seeking protection from the heavy fire that descended on what remained of the column. They acted individually; no orders were coming from the top. The shock of a disrupted offensive was still setting in.

Sunshine began to filter through the smoke over Dong Ha. In the distance Ripley heard the droning of Vietnamese A-1 Skyraiders, Spads, coming from the south. As they passed overhead, two of them, another wave of cheering broke from the Soi Bien.

The Spads wasted no time. The lead aircraft rolled in hot, with firing switches activated, while the wingman took up a racetrack pattern aloft. From the higher altitude he could follow the entire run of the first plane, watch for signs of gunfire or some other reaction from the ground, and calculate the effects of the initial attack, making his own run against another target if the first were destroyed.

How can they miss? thought Ripley. If they hit anywhere near the road they're bound to get an armored vehicle or troops clustered nearby. Then a high-pitched whine jolted him. It was the sound of motors on the tracking radars of vehicle-mounted antiaircraft guns, ZSU 23–24s. Deadly.

Near the bottom of its dive, the lead aircraft launched a rocket from under a wing and produced a near-instantaneous fireball that engulfed one of the tanks. The Spad's laydown speed was leisurely, deceptively so; it was hard to lead with a shoulder weapon and the infantry fire rattling skyward was ineffectual. Nor did the ZSUs fire. Maybe they haven't got the command yet, he thought. He was still afraid for the second pilot.

As the first Spad clawed its way back to altitude for another pass at the tanks, the second rolled in on its target. A small, brilliant flash lit up the north bank. But the second rocket hadn't been fired. What's happening? he wondered. Then he saw a thin pencil of light shooting skyward, straight for the diving Spad. It penetrated the aircraft's belly and exploded deep inside.

"Je-sus Christ!" he said, more to himself than Nha, the only person nearby. Surface-to-air missile, man-packed. "It's a Strella, isn't it?" Nha, not understanding the new word, didn't answer.

So the Soviets had supplied their clients with the new SAM. That changed things. The South Vietnamese wouldn't get much close air support, not in a hot missile zone like this.

The stricken Spad lurched, then began to spin toward the ground, trailing black smoke. A thousand feet up a parachute blossomed. The pilot dangled from the harness directly over the river, drifting southward. He'd be on the ground in less than a minute.

But when he was halfway down the wind shifted toward the north. The pilot pulled on his parachute's risers, trying to slip into the wind and slow the rate of drift. There was no ground fire from the north bank and it was evident to Ripley that the NVA wanted the man alive. As he descended to treetop level, troops surged toward the anticipated landing point.

On the south bank the Marines, yelling encouragement before, fell silent. The moat worked to the enemy's advantage as well as their own. There was no way to save the pilot.

The other Spad made one last helpless circle at high altitude before heading south. He knew he had no chance against the Strella.

The euphoria of deliverance faded quickly on the south bank. By sunset the North Vietnamese were beginning to move again. They searched along the river between the destroyed highway bridge and the railroad bridge upstream—scene of that morning's failed assault—for alternate crossing sites. Firefights erupted throughout the night. NVA infantry probed Binh's line for gaps through which they could infiltrate, outflank, or overwhelm Soi Bien defensive positions. Binh's Marines managed to counter each new attack.

Shortly before midnight Ripley heard the cough and rumble of tanks starting up, followed by the squeaking of roadwheels as they began to move west along the north bank, toward Cam Lo. It sounded like at least twenty. They were probably looking for a shallow place to ford the river.

It was time to call the Navy again. Nha gave him the handset and within minutes the first salvo from an offshore destroyer screamed over Dong Ha and landed five hundred yards upstream. A tank near the head of the column erupted in flames, illuminating other tanks as they tried to get past it. Now he could see well enough to act as a gunfire spotter. The destroyer's guns were already shooting along the NVA column's axis of advance. Fire simply had to be walked upstream at the speed of the tanks.

"Add five-zero and fire for effect," Ripley said. "Keep adding and firing until I send the cease-fire or they roll out of your range. You're moving right along with them."

Heavy, high-velocity fire started from the high ground behind him. Smock had evidently talked Ley into moving some tanks on line and they were trying to stop the NVA column with direct fire. They continued to fire and score hits until the column had moved past the last burning tank and into the darkness. The destroyer walked its fire along the riverbank for another twenty minutes or so, then radioed that the target was beyond maximum range.

By daybreak, none of the NVA tanks had made it to Cam Lo and the infantry had been unable to cross the Cua Viet in force. The situation is stabilizing, Ripley thought. Then Brigade radioed; Nha ran up with the antenna waving. "Bad news, Delta. The Fourth Battalion, what's left of it, is straggling back from Sarge and Nui Ba Ho. They're down to one hundred fifty men, but both *co-van*s are okay."

Then Brigade radioed again. "ExO of the Fifty-Sixth ARVN surrendered Camp Carroll without a shot being fired. The CO was too weak to stop him."

After Ripley had given the handset back to Nha, he sat on the ground and gripped his head with the palms of his hands. So this was what it had come to. The very moment Binh had been issuing his fight-until-death order to the Soi Bien, the Fifty-Sixth ARVN were stacking arms and hauling down their colors. Almost all the way to the top, South Vietnam-ese were deserting. The gate had been thrown open for an NVA advance from the west.

TWELVE

For several days, Dong Ha and its immediate surroundings held fast while South Vietnamese positions to the south and west crumbled. Then, four days after Ripley had cut the highway structure, enemy troops were attacking across the river in the vicinity of the damaged railroad bridge. The Soi Bien were dug in along both sides of a pagoda, poised for a counterattack. Highway 9 and the Dong Ha cemetery lay behind them. Protecting the flanks of their position were some of Ley's tanks and armored personnel carriers.

"Nha," Ripley said, and his radio operator gave him the handset. The two of them had been passing it back and forth as Ripley made desperate calls for naval gunfire and artillery support.

A vehicle swerved up to the pagoda and skidded to a stop. Five journalists and two cameramen jumped out. In clean clothes, freshly shaven, they converged on Ripley with microphones.

"Are you the Marine captain who blew up the bridge?"

"You're big-time copy back home, Captain. Where are you from?"

"What's going on? Will we stop the NVA here? Can they cross somewhere else?"

He pulled back from the microphones. The Soi Bien hadn't opened fire yet; evidently the newsmen didn't know what was about to happen. "I advise you to leave, now," he said. But they remained, closing in on him, the cameramen filming a few yards away.

Then the calm was shattered by a series of sharp cracks and the ground around them erupted in geysers of dirt and black smoke. Mortar rounds.

"Get the hell out of here, they're attacking!" Ripley yelled.

Instead they pressed closer, blocking his vision so that he couldn't adjust the return fire. He raised his arm to sweep them aside when the earth shook and a huge force drove them all to the ground. The newsmen lay in a pile on top of him, suddenly silent.

He worked his way out of the bodies as some of them started to writhe and groan. Blood spurted from the neck of one of the cameramen, covering those beneath him.

They're either dead or badly wounded, all of them, Ripley thought. They're not moving much.

Then he saw someone lying off to the side. Nha, he realized, a heavy, fearful sensation in his stomach. He turned the body over. Yes. A single flying fragment had sheared off the radio antenna and driven into his skull just below the helmet. *Anh nho!* Nha, his little brother, dead.

He was alone now. He looked around wildly. There, less than fifty yards away, Smock was crumpled on the ground, wounded. Ripley ran to him. Only four days earlier the three of them had brought down that monster bridge and run through heavy enemy fire getting to and from it and they'd come out alive because they were invulnerable. Now Nha lay dead and Smock was bleeding. The whole crazy notion of invulnerability went flowing away with his blood.

He felt as though for the past few days he'd been on a painkiller that was just beginning to wear off. Sweet Jesus! Nha gone, Smock about to be. What do I do now? he thought.

Then he saw the South Vietnamese tanks and armored vehicles turning around, moving away from the incoming fire. They weren't going to stop to pick up casualties on the way out.

"*Dung lai!* Halt, you rotten sonofabitch!" Ripley screamed at the closest tank.

The tanker continued to roll away but the nearest armored personnel carrier stopped, possibly because the driver understood some English.

"Look, man, they're hurt bad," Ripley said. "We have to get them to a doctor."

The driver lowered the ramp in the rear and Ripley hauled Smock and another wounded tank battalion advisor on board. When he was going back for Nha and the wounded journalists, the driver closed the ramp and sent the tracked vehicle lurching forward. Ripley ran alongside, waving and shouting, but it gained speed. And then another mortar round exploded nearby.

It knocked him into a ditch, where he lay for a few minutes stunned but unhurt. By the time he crawled out, the rest of the tanks and personnel carriers had left. Even defending infantry units had pulled back to escape the indirect fire now blanketing the area.

He'd been left behind. With the corpse of his most loyal friend, seven wounded newsmen, and a radio without an antenna.

Seconds later, a lone South Vietnamese tank rumbled out of the haze and headed east along Highway 9. The hatch was open and the driver's head was visible. Ripley ran to the center of the road. He held his carbine high with both hands, signaling the driver to stop, but he wouldn't. So Ripley lowered the carbine and took careful aim at his head. The tank stopped then, and the crew set about stacking the wounded newsmen around the turret. Ripley moved off to retrieve Nha's body. He had just slung it over his shoulder and was heading back when the tank started moving. It accelerated rapidly and barreled away.

Ripley cursed. Now what? He couldn't leave Nha behind, and without an antenna he couldn't use Nha's radio to get help. Maybe there was another radio lying around. He set Nha down and searched. Within minutes he found a dead Vietnamese radioman. The force of an exploding mortar round had flung his backpack and radio several feet away, but the equipment appeared to be intact.

Bending over to detach the antenna, he heard something move. He glanced up and saw that the point men of several NVA rifle squads were crossing Highway 9 toward him. Other soldiers were approaching through the trees of the nearby graveyard. They carried assault rifles at the ready, with curved banana magazines inserted. They looked like ghosts coming through the smoke and they were as quiet as he imagined ghosts would be. Not one of them spoke.

So this is how it's going to end, he thought. Not blown sky-high by an exploding bridge, not tearing through a hail of fire with the Soi Bien cheering me on, but here, alone, in a ghost town, trying to unscrew an antenna from a dead man's radio. It seemed absurd, and yet somehow strangely appropriate. He felt as if somewhere inside him he had known all his life that it would end just like this, right here, right now, not in splendor but in silence.

He was going to die. He was going to die and it didn't make any difference how, whether he would get shot in the chest or the back. They'd have to shoot him in the back because he was taking Nha as far away as he could before the bullets caught him. He had to leave with Nha, even if he only made it two feet down the road. Suddenly, this seemed as important to him as blowing the bridge had four days earlier.

He shouldered the body again and started walking toward the railroad embankment. Nha's head lolled indolently against his back as he moved along. He heard the clicking of safety catches being taken off. Yes, he would get it in the back. Just a couple of thumps, knocking the wind out of him. He might even be dead before it started to hurt.

"*Dai-uy!*" someone yelled. He looked up. Three-Finger Jack and another bodyguard were on top of the embankment directly in front of him. They opened fire on the advancing troops and drove them to the ground. More Marines appeared alongside the bodyguards and together they built up a heavy base of fire, keeping the enemy pinned down while Ripley struggled up the embankment, Nha's dead weight on his shoulders.

He was safe. Alive. He saw now how wrong he had been, to think his end was predestined to take place here, now, as wrong as he had been four days earlier thinking some supernatural shield protected

him when he went running uphill from the bridge. He had slipped past death one more time, not because of any shield but because of Jack, who prized honor and loyalty above all.

Life hung on such a slender thread: the silken filament a spider suddenly drops from. He thought of all the people he cared most about. His wife and children. Binh, vulnerable. Smock, cocky once, now badly wounded. His little brother Nha, dead. And not far away on the embankment, expressionless Jack.

"*Gia cam on,*" Ripley called. Thanks, buddy. And, for the first time, he saw the bodyguard's face open up in an unrestrained smile. Reason had told him he would never understand this man, his language, his history, the loyalty he had shown to Binh and now, just as intensely, to him. But for one moment that changed. The world seemed to come to a stop; all its energy and light turned toward Jack, illuminating the lines in his face, and Ripley saw him as if not an inch of space stood between them. The stillness and clarity washed all reason away. There was no past and no future, no subject and no object, no difference between him and Three-Finger Jack.

Within days, the North Vietnamese had pinched off the Dong Ha salient at its base south of town. By the time the Third Marine Battalion received orders to break through the encircling enemy, its strength had dwindled to two hundred fighters, including the walking wounded. All of Lieutenant Colonel Ley's tanks had been lost, to either battle damage or lack of fuel and ammunition. So the tankers picked up rifles and fought as infantrymen alongside the Soi Bien. A few weeks later, after more bitter fighting near Quang Tri City, the battalion was pulled out of the line.

At its first formation back at Hue, he stood beside Binh, in front of three ragged ranks. Nearly all the Marines he'd been close to were missing at that morning's muster. Out of a battalion of seven hundred men, there were only fifty-two survivors. The two rifle companies defending the south bank of the Cua Viet, the Marines who covered him and Smock while they rigged the bridge for destruction, had perished to a man.

*C*aptain Rip-
ley's year-long tour as a *co-van* ended in early June.
He spent a week in Saigon getting ready for his freedom flight back to the United States. The city still
showed no sense of urgency. The Easter Offensive
had been stalled and no other major threats appeared. Most of the Vietnamese Marine Division remained in the north. Saigon headquarters kept in
touch with two radio calls each day, a schedule ob-

served as religiously as the daily volleyball game in the courtyard.

On the morning of his departure, Ripley packed the most serviceable of his tiger suits, thin and faded, and discarded the rest. Then he dressed carefully in his grease suit, the one he saved for ceremonies and inspections. He had one final call to make.

During the jeep ride to Di An, a Marine base camp with a community of dependents living nearby, he rehearsed his speech. He had an interpreter as backup; this was too important to leave to chance. When they got to the house the interpreter called softly and a woman came out, followed by four boys. The tallest could not have been more than ten years old. Ripley spoke and during the translation the woman looked at him intently, but without comprehension. There would be no reply. He pulled out a roll of Vietnamese money he had saved and handed the bills to the oldest boy, then bowed slightly to the mother and left.

The gravesite was easy to find. Mounds of freshly turned earth dotted the unshaded field. Waves of heat shimmered near the ground. Insects droned in the background, an occasional bird sang out, but otherwise the silence was complete. They searched for several minutes and then found a wooden marker. The interpreter, reading the name, showed new respect. "This very good Marine. He not die easy."

Jack's end had come sometime around midnight. After the breakout from Dong Ha, the Third Battalion had taken up defensive positions around the combat base at Ai Tu. Two rifle companies were withdrawing behind friendly lines under pressure from a larger NVA force. Binh and Ripley led reinforcements into no-man's land. Both of them talked on their radios, maneuvering the beleaguered companies and coaxing fire support from Brigade.

To signal a final assault on the retreating Southerners, the North Vietnamese sent up a white flare, revealing the long antennas of Binh's command group to an NVA platoon a hundred yards away. As the flare burned out, three Marines rushed past Binh and Ripley to meet the advancing enemy head on. Several others, invisible, reached through the darkness to pull the commander and the *co-van* to safety inside the tactical wire.

They couldn't see the hand-to-hand combat outside the wire but they could hear it. At first light they found the three Marines in contorted postures, stiffening in death. Two or three dozen enemy soldiers were heaped around them. Three-Finger Jack lay half covered by the body of the Northerner who had managed to kill him. Jack held his carbine in one hand, his fighting knife in the other.

At the cemetery Captain Ripley asked the interpreter to leave him for a moment. Reaching into a small canvas bag, he brought out a bloodstained fighting knife that had been pried from the dead Marine's hand. He dug a small hole in the mound of earth over the grave and placed the knife inside. Pushing the dirt back in the hole, he patted it smooth and stood for a final salute to the knife's owner—the man who had carried out his vow to die for Binh, and who had risked his life for Ripley.

Captain Ripley's sense of loss and frustration was shared by many *co-vans* as they left Vietnam in those final years. Though relieved to be walking away intact from a year of combat service, they knew that they were leaving their Vietnamese Marine brothers behind to fight for their lives. How much longer could the South Vietnamese continue? Where would they get other Nhas, other Jacks? Would the enemy ever stop trying to conquer the South?

Early in May the Third ARVN Division reconstituted a defensive line along the My Chanh River, south of Quang Tri. They vowed that the line would never be crossed. It wasn't, that summer anyway. In July, supported by amphibian tractors and helicopters of the U.S. Special Landing Force, the Marines, with the airborne division, counterattacked north across the My Chanh and in time recaptured what was left of Quang Tri.

Thus the Easter Offensive was stopped, far short of its objective. The NVA's failure to cross the bridge at Dong Ha had led to bloody stalemate. In Hanoi, a frustrated North Vietnamese politburo reviewed the situation. They concluded that General Vo Nguyen Giap—victor over the French at Dien Bien Phu, minister of defense throughout the war with the Americans, and architect of the 1972 Easter Offensive— would have to be removed from power. They would

not stop trying, no matter what cease-fire agree-
ments might come into effect. But it would take years
to regroup and prepare another invasion on such a
grand scale.

Three years, to be exact.

ACKNOWLEDGMENTS

*O*bviously, this book required the total participation of Colonel John W. Ripley, U.S. Marine Corps, who had to reach back and retrieve many long-forgotten details, some quite painful, to re-create his ordeal at Dong Ha. His charming wife Molin helped keep the manuscript moving and was a valued cheerleader and counselor throughout the project. I am also indebted to my good friend and neighbor, Jayne Karsten, for her expert advice on early drafts and her undiminished enthusiasm from beginning to end. At the U.S. Naval Academy, Midshipman First Class Tung X. Pham gave the text a needed scrub from the Vietnamese perspective. And at the Naval Institute Press, Tom Epley and Deborah Estes were the first to see the manuscript's potential despite a rough first draft. From the managing editor's desk Laurie Stearns offered much-needed encouragement during later drafts, and from Montreal, manuscript editor Connie Buchanan solved several knotty technical problems and proved once again that first-rate editing requires equal amounts of brilliance and diligence.

Heartfelt thanks also go to my wife Susan for her unlimited patience and for the skill she exercised more than once in keeping the story of Ripley at the bridge from being dumped down the memory hole of our home computer.

A final acknowledgment must go to the men who wore the tiger suits—the *co-van*s—and who, with their brothers-in-arms, upheld a proud fighting tradition to the bitter end.

The Naval Institute Press is the book-publishing arm of the U.S. Naval Institute, a private, nonprofit professional society for members of the sea services and civilians who share an interest in naval and maritime affairs. Established in 1873 at the U.S. Naval Academy in Annapolis, Maryland, where its offices remain today, the Naval Institute has more than 100,000 members worldwide.

Members of the Naval Institute receive the influential monthly naval magazine *Proceedings* and substantial discounts on fine nautical prints, ship and aircraft photos, and subscriptions to the Institute's recently inaugurated quarterly, *Naval History.* They also have access to the transcripts of the Institute's Oral History Program and may attend any of the Institute-sponsored seminars regularly offered around the country.

The book-publishing program, begun in 1898 with basic guides to naval practices, has broadened its scope in recent years to include books of more general interest. Now the Naval Institute Press publishes more than forty new titles each year, ranging from how-to books on boating and navigation to battle histories, biographies, ship guides, and novels. Institute members receive discounts on the Press's more than 300 books.

For a free catalog describing books currently available and for further information about U.S. Naval Institute membership, please write to:

Membership Department
U.S. Naval Institute
Annapolis, Maryland 21402

or call, toll-free, 800-233-USNI.